A French Garden

The

Loire Valley

Revised Edition

K. B. Oliver

Also by K. B. Oliver

Books

Magical Paris: Over 100 Things to Do Across Paris

A French Garden: The Loire Valley

Real French for Travelers

Resources

Real French for Travelers Complete Online Course

www.realfrenchfortravelers.com

Oliver's France Website (for a wealth of travel ideas) and a free online mini course on greetings and polite French expressions. Oliversfrance.com

2022 Introduction in a Post-Covid France

Travel is back! And France has opened its doors for you!

What has changed since pre-Covid? In updating this book, I have found some changes in hours, slight or no changes in most admission prices, and almost nothing permanently closed, aside from a few restaurants. France in general no longer requires masks or proof of vaccination, except in public transportation and in healthcare establishments as of March 14, 2022. It's best to be prepared and have a mask available in case smaller venues require them or if you find yourself in close quarters and feel more at ease. (A *pass sanitaire* is a vaccine pass.) Things change quickly, so be sure to check online right before your trip, so there are no surprises.

Bon Voyage!

K. B. Oliver

Table of Contents

Why You Want to Go to the Loire Valley

Ici, vivre c'est un art

Here, Living is an Art (Loire Valley Tourism Slogan)

The Loire Valley . . . What images come to your mind? Waves of green fields woven with gnarly grapevines, a wide, peaceful river flowing through a pastoral countryside, regal white castles, their towers and turrets visible from a distance? As the above French tourism slogan attests, life is an art form here. Your idyllic images will become reality as you make your way to this magical place.

The lush Loire River valley sits alongside the Loire River, which peacefully meanders westward to the Atlantic Ocean. The river divides France roughly in half across the middle. Over 600 miles long, the longest river in France, the Loire River snakes north then veers west to the Atlantic Ocean, with smaller rivers branching outward like life-giving arteries.

It's no coincidence that this fertile swath of land is called the garden of France. And like a bountiful garden, life is tranquil here. Towns bustle, filled with open markets, shops, ancient walls, medieval castles. These towns are smaller than the big urban centers of France, but as vibrant and appealing, offering plenty to do and see. The land is generally flat, perfect for hiking and biking. This calm region in central France is worth discovering.

Many people aren't quite sure where the Loire Valley is located or what attractions it holds. Or if they have heard of it, they know only of the castles, but not the myriad other activities and treasures that await those who visit. In addition to touring the stunning castles, which, of course, you'll want to do, there are many other sights and experiences to enjoy.

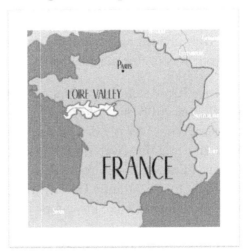

The Loire Valley is under two hours from Paris by the TGV train, so it is convenient as a side trip from the capital, even if you have only 2 or 3 days. (A short side trip itinerary is suggested later in the book.) With a dozen daily trains to the region, it is easy to get there. By car it isn't very far, either.

The most striking feature of the Loire Valley is the presence of châteaux, clues of the area's noble and opulent past. There are about 1,000 of them, all with varying ages and degrees of ruin or elegance. Some are tourist destinations, others are hotels, and still others, abandoned medieval fortresses. They are the magnets that draw the majority of visitors to the area.

Some guidebooks devote most of their text to the châteaux, but in this guide, you'll find that plus much more, a broad spectrum of activities for both nature-lovers and city-hoppers. You'll find the basics of what you need, not a lot of things you don't need. If you want to simplify your understanding of the region, plan your trip without getting a headache, yet still taste the main attractions *and* the quirky or lesser-known destinations, this book is a good choice.

Maybe you have a castle list. You'd like to see a varied assortment, from crumbling medieval relics of history to pristine, fairytale-like visions. Perhaps vineyards and wine-tasting are your interest. The

Loire Valley is one of the most important wine regions in France, and even the world. Maybe you dream of flying in a hot-air balloon over the valley, seeing its wonders from high altitude. Or maybe a visit to a cave dwelling, a zoo, or a mushroom farm sounds like fun . . . there is something for everyone in the Loire Valley. You don't have to choose only one favorite destination or activity, because everything's linked by an easy drive or train ride.

A Majestic River

The Loire River is the spinal cord of the Loire Valley, supplying life to the surrounding region for past centuries. Dozens of tributaries branch off to form smaller rivers. From the beginning of the river near Valence in the southern part of France, much of it actually flows north. Once it reaches Orléans, it veers west and flows toward the Atlantic Ocean, near Nantes. This expanse between the towns of Orléans and Nantes is the area we know as the Loire Valley and is about 170 miles in length.

For nearly two centuries from as early as 600 B. C., the Loire was a main trading route to move goods around the country. In the 19th century when railroads were built, trade shifted away from the river.

In the first century B.C., the Romans "adopted" this area, as they did much of France, and planted vineyards. Today it is one of the major wine-producing regions in the country. In 2002 the Loire River Valley was named by UNESCO as a world heritage site.

Once Upon a Time...

What we see today in the Loire Valley has its roots in a spectacular military defeat during the Hundred Years War between France and England. The year was 1415. Henry V of England soundly defeated France in the Battle of Agincourt and became the regent of France, as well as heir to the throne. France's king, Charles VII, fled Paris to the Loire Valley, followed by many other French nobles. The city of Orléans was later delivered from the English by Joan of Arc.

Once things settled down (and France was once again French), many of the exiles to the Loire decided to stay there, since the land was fertile, and the river provided easy transport of goods to many parts of the country. Later, during the Renaissance, the architectural revolution began, and many castles were built or restored. What was once a haven of exiles became the luxurious "suburbs" of Paris, even after the seat of government returned to Paris. At one time both Tours and Orléans were larger and more important than Paris.

In the early 16th century, King François I invited the elderly Leonardo da Vinci to resettle in France following the death of his patron. The artist agreed, bringing the Mona Lisa with him. François I gave him a generous allowance and a château to live in, Clos Lucé. Eventually the French monarchy returned to Paris, but the area continued to thrive, thanks to the textile industry, agriculture, and an increase in the number of Catholic institutions in the area. This development skidded abruptly to a stop when the French Revolution erupted. During that time and afterward, many châteaux fell into neglect, or had parts sold off, some never to be restored.

During World War I, this area was again a center of government, while World War II saw Nazi occupation. Following the wars, the Valley gradually healed and began to grow as a major tourist destination in France. Today this trend continues as the Loire Valley's popularity flourishes.

The Valley Awaits You

As mentioned, the Loire River Valley extends about 170 miles east and west through the center of France, from the eastern city of Orleans westward to Angers and on to the Atlantic. The distance between these cities is about 140 miles. There is an enormous amount to discover between (and including) these two cities!

In a few more pages you'll see a map showing the entire area divided into four sections. Depending on how much time you have, you can choose a base city in one of these sections, explore the surrounding area, and move on from there. Each area will be explained with logistical helps as well as things to do. There is a lot to do and see in each section, aside from châteaux. In each section you'll find some suggestions for hotels and restaurants. On pages 161-162 there is a list of châteaux that have been transformed into hotels. So, if your dream is to stay in a château, that section is your resource!

How to use this book This guide is divided into several helpful sections. It is designed to be **easy to use** so you can quickly find what you need *before* and *during* your trip. To the extent possible, each site is arranged in proximity to others you'll want to visit so you can make the best use of your time, gas, and shoe leather.

1. **Part One: Let's Get Practical**
    This section will give you the overview of the Loire Valley and a map of the area so you can get oriented. There are also practical details to help you prepare and make sure your trip goes as smoothly as possible, and you don't miss anything you really want to see!

You'll find more in-depth descriptions of each area in the corresponding parts of the book.

2. **Part Two: All Over the Valley** will give you detailed information about things to see and do (look for the heading, **Seeing and Doing**) as well as lodging and restaurant options (see the heading **Staying and Eating**.) In Part Two of the book there are five sections (beginning with the city of Tours and moving clockwise) according to the following geographical areas:

The City of Tours is the largest city in the Valley, as well as the geographical center of the region. This city has its own section since it is right in the middle of the Loire Valley and has enough going on to merit its own chapter. It makes a good base city if you want a bigger town experience and plan to fan out east and west across the Valley.

The Northeast, which includes the cities of Amboise and Blois along with many châteaux and activities there.

The Southeast, including the town of Loches and its castle.

The Southwest, including the towns of Saumur and Chinon.

The Northwest, including the city of Angers.

3. **Part Three: More Fun in the Valley**
   This section will provide resources for special
   themes, such as nature activities and specialties
   of food and wine that the Loire Valley is known
   for. A helpful castle chart provides a brief
   description of the features of each château, to help
   you choose which ones you want to see. You'll
   even find a list of châteaux-hotels to top off your
   castle-hopping experience!

4. **Part Four: Suggested Itineraries** Lastly,
   you'll find a list of Suggested itineraries,
   organized both by the length of time you have
   available and by theme. If you have more time,
   you could combine two or more of the suggested
   itineraries.

In each geographical section covered, be sure to look
for the general headings: ***Seeing and Doing***,
which covers activities and interesting sites, and the
heading ***Staying and Eating***, which covers
suggested hotels and restaurants. These are just a
small sampling of the many options for hotels and
restaurants that exist in these areas.

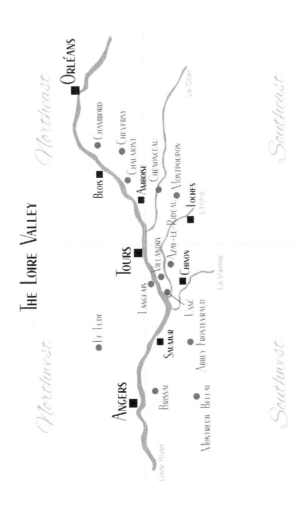

The Loire Valley

Orléans
Chambord
Cheverny
Chaumont
Blois
Chenonceau
Amboise
Montpoupon
Loches
Azay-le-Rideau
Tours
Villandry
Chinon
Langeais
Ussé
Le Cher
L'Indre
La Vienne
Il Lude
Saumur
Abbey Fontevraud
Angers
Brissac
Montreuil Bellay
Loire River

Northwest
Northeast
Southwest
Southeast

Let's Get Practical

Getting to France

Although there are major airports in the Loire Valley, you may find the most reasonable rates for flights will take you into Paris. From there you can take the high-speed train, the TGV, and be in the Loire Valley in about an hour and a half. This is especially helpful if you want to visit Paris then the Loire Valley, or vice versa. If you want to rent a car, you can do that at any train station in larger cities, such as Angers or Tours. Otherwise, you can rent a car at the Paris airport and head down the A10 autoroute toward the city of Orléans. The A11 autoroute forks to the west in the direction of Angers.

Once you are in the Loire Valley, if you have a car, you'll find the D952 route is scenic, as it follows along the river from east to west.

When to Go

Temperatures in the Loire Valley begin to warm up in April (average low 50s) and are comfortable until October. The warmest months are in summer, June through August, but even then, they remain comfortable. The highest rainfall is in May. June through September have the most hours of sunlight.

If you go too early (April, early May), you won't see all of the flowers in bloom in châteaux gardens, for example, in Villandry, which has one of the most sumptuous gardens in the Loire Valley. Crowds will be thinner at that time, though.

Keep in mind that the Loire Valley has become very popular with travelers from around the world, including the French. You'll need to make your reservations several months early if you want good choices, better prices, and less stress.

Getting around

To get around once you are *in* the Loire Valley, you have several options. If you choose to rent a car, you'll have easy access to pretty much everything, since nearly anything you want to visit is only a short distance away. Cars are available at airports, most train stations of larger towns, and often elsewhere in the town itself. You'll likely save money, though, if you book online. And of course, you'll want to reserve well in advance, though it isn't necessarily impossible to get a car on a whim. Just check. During a visit to Tours, I decided on the spur of the moment to rent a car for a day to see a few places I hadn't yet seen and was able to get one at the Tours train station. It's possible, but better to reserve in advance.

For all the convenience of renting a car, there is the matter of planning routes and finding your way. If this is not your favorite thing to do, you might like to book an organized tour or combine driving on your own to certain places with letting someone else do the driving for others. You'll find many companies to choose from (pages 46-47), usually taking you to your destination in vans or smaller vehicles. You can plan your entire trip as a package, or you can visit specific places à la carte with a company, while leaving other days open to organize yourself.

A third option is to take a train or a bus from one city to another. This works well if you are aiming for larger towns or better-known châteaux where there will be bus, train, or tour services to those locations. It will be a bit more difficult if you want to visit, for example, a small family-owned vineyard out in the countryside. For that, it would be best to have a rental car. That being said, there are also vineyard tours available in small groups, so the lack of a car shouldn't stop you from doing most of what you want to do.

Some bus routes could be less frequent in the summer, though train routes will still work. The problem with trains is that you'll have to organize around their timetable. This will cost you more time getting to and from your destination than if you have a car. Routes and hours of both trains and buses will be available at train stations or tourist bureaus.

If you are traveling by train, you can get a booklet, *Les Chateaux de la Loire en Train* (the Loire Valley Châteaux by Train), at the train station, which will give you the lowdown on travel to and from your destinations. Otherwise, every train station should have small brochures with timetables between destinations, both going and returning. Usually, the longest you'd spend in a train will be 2 hours or so if you want to travel from one end to the other.

Phone numbers listed in the book will be local numbers. If using an international phone, add 33 and omit 0.

All Over the Valley

Tours

Tours is the largest city destination in the Loire Valley. It is often called the gateway to the Loire Valley, because it neatly divides the east and west sides of the 170-mile-long stretch, making it a great jumping-off point for castle or vineyard-hopping. Nearby châteaux and excursions all along the Loire Valley are easy to access with a short drive or train hop, as nine million tourists per year have discovered. Despite the convenient centrality of Tours as a base, you won't want to neglect a visit to the bustling city itself.

The city of Tours sits between two rivers, the Loire and the Cher. You can get to the city from Paris in about an hour or so on the fast train, and there are several of these per day. This makes the Loire Valley a great side trip *or* final destination. You can also get there on a TGV high-speed train directly from the Charles de Gaulle Airport in Paris.

Once you are in Tours, you'll feel the city energy, but still be able to breathe in the peaceful, relaxed pace one typically finds in the towns and villages of central France. Tours is small enough to be walkable or easily accessible by tram, and large enough to exude a lively ambiance that offers plenty to see and do.

The city's population is around 140,000, about 40,000 of whom are college students, adding youthful energy to the city atmosphere. Many of them hang out on Rue Colbert, where you'll find a variety of budget-friendly restaurants.

Tours has another nickname, "little Paris." Many of the buildings resemble those in Paris, such as the Belle Epoch Hôtel de Ville, or city hall. It was built by a native Tours architect, Victor Laloux, who also designed the Tours train station, as well as another famous train station which eventually became the Musée d'Orsay in Paris.

In Tours, supposedly the purest French is spoken, although many towns in the center of France make this claim. So, if you are studying French and want to learn a good accent, this is your place.

The Tourist Information Bureau is about a 10-minute walk from the train station. This is a strategic place to begin your exploration of the city. You can also get all kinds of information about tours, housing, activities, and much more for the entire region. Of course, you'll want to start with a city map, which is a good practice that can orient you, no matter where you are going. The Tourist Bureau address is 78-82 rue Bernard Palissy. www.tours-tourisme.fr.

A map, or *plan de ville*, will show you the layout of the city and where the Old Town is located, on the left bank of the river. This corner of Tours is one you'll likely want to visit, with its picturesque squares, surrounded by 14th to 16th century half-timbered buildings, cafés, and shops. The sprawling urban area flows out on both sides of the river.

Medieval Buildings in Old Tours

While you are at the Tourist Bureau, ask about guided tours of the Old City. These are in English on Wednesdays. Otherwise, there are tours in French on most Sundays and some Saturdays. Hour and a half tours are 6€ for adults and 3€ for children 12 to 18 years old. There are many thematic tours that you can book (cathedrals, art, history), though most of these are in French. While at the Bureau, you can also find out about museum passes, which give you access to several popular museums for one price. Also, you can learn where the city tramlines go and how to use them. That may help when your feet become tired! https://www.filbleu.fr/en/timetable-journey/maps

Next to the Tourism Bureau and near the train station is the modern Vinci Conference Center, which has an interesting architectural design. *See other practical tips at the end of this chapter.*

A Look Backward in History The first inhabitants of Tours, a Gallic people called the Turones, settled on the right bank of the river. Later in the first century, the Romans arrived and moved them to the left bank, calling the city Caesarodunum. In the year 732, The Battle of Tours was fought against the Moors, and Charles Martel pushed back Islam from France. This battle is sometimes called the Battle of Poitiers (since the battle occurred between Tours and Poitiers) but is not to be confused with another battle by that name during the Hundred Years War with England, in 1356.

In the 3rd century, this settlement was Christianized by St. Gatien. You can see the impressive Gothic cathedral in his name on your way to the Old Town. A century later, St. Martin continued this work to an even greater extent. The basilica built on his tomb in the 5th century attracted pilgrims for centuries and brought growth to the town.

In the 6th century St. Gregory of Tours had an abbey built around the basilica. It was damaged or destroyed several times (see St. Martin Basilica) and restored much later in the late 19th century by, once again, architect Victor Laloux.

In the 15th and 16th centuries, Tours was the capital of France. During that time the city flourished in the arts, in architecture, and in economic development (including a thriving silk industry.) In the 18th century, the city underwent its own urban renewal, which replaced the "medieval disorder", as it was called, with beautified streets and neighborhoods. The city grew in population and prosperity, despite the later struggles of the French Revolution and two World Wars, the second of which destroyed a quarter of the city. In the 60s, Tours was again restored and upgraded. During that process, care was taken to preserve its medieval charm.

Seeing and Doing in Tours

You will likely spend most of your time in Tours on the western bank of the Loire, where you'll find the Old Town (Vieux Tours) and the Cathedral district, as well as all the cobbled and paved avenues that connect them.

Rue Nationale is a wide avenue running from the left (southern) riverbank going south, dividing this section of the city in half. Shops line either side of this thoroughfare and there is a north-south tram line as well. The northern point of Rue Nationale leads to the Pont (bridge) Wilson. To the south it dead ends at the Place Jean Jaurès and the Boulevard Béranger, with the city hall to one side, the Palais de Justice (courthouse) on the other. It's a lovely area, with fountains and flowerbeds all around.

Since Rue Nationale cuts through the middle of this part of Tours, we'll first cover the area *west* of Rue Nationale (as you are facing the Loire to the north), then we'll go *east* of Rue Nationale. Lastly, the guide will take you to the city hall and east-west Boulevard Béranger (which turns into Boulevard Heurteloup as you go east.)

West of Rue Nationale

To the west of Rue Nationale close to the river is Vieux Tours, or the Old Town. The heart of Vieux Tours is the **Place Plumereau.** The *Place* is surrounded by half-timbered houses and other late-medieval buildings, as well as shops, cafés, and restaurants. From there you can wander through numerous narrow streets and marvel at medieval architecture towering over you, imagining a 15th century family coming and going out of one of the homes. A main east-west street is Rue du Commerce, where you'll join the crowds listening to street entertainment, browsing shops, or looking for good Loire Valley cuisine or a drink.

Place Plumereau

As you wander south from there, you will encounter the **Basilique St. Martin** and the **Musée St. Martin.** This esteemed gentleman, St. Martin, was mentioned in the historical summary of Tours. The Basilica has a long, complex history, but its existence was a key part of the growth and importance of the city.

Originally built in 466 on St. Martin's grave, a larger version of the church was constructed in 1014. This burned down in 1230 and later in the 13th century a Romanesque Basilica was erected to replace it. It was this huge and impressive church that drew pilgrims from all over France. It was considered one of the most important sites of pilgrimage at the time.

During the Wars of Religion, it was partly damaged by Huguenots and later the job was completed during the French Revolution. All that remained were two towers, **Tour Charlemagne** and **Tour de l'Horloge** (clock tower), which you can see nearby. Finally, in 1860 excavations indicated where the church had been, and a new basilica was commissioned. This last version was designed by Victor Laloux and you can visit it, as well as the St. Martin Museum.

Saint Martin Museum Learn more about the man whose life and work changed the religious face of Tours. See frescos of the Charlemagne Tower, murals, and sculptures.

Address: 3 Rue Rapin in the 13th century St Jean Chapel.

Hours: Open mid-March to mid-November from Wednesday to Sunday, 9:30 am to 1, 2 to 5:30.

Admission: 2 €.

Moving north toward the river, you'll encounter a 15th century mansion that was once a private home, the **Hôtel Goüin**, named after the Goüin family, wealthy bankers from Brittany, who purchased it in 1738. (Often a private mansion was called a "hôtel".) During the Second World War, the house was destroyed, all except for the magnificent 16th century façade. Today it is a museum with exhibits of art and objects. In the basement there are Gallo-Roman ruins.

Address: 25 Rue du Commerce.

Admission: Free

Nearby the Goüin House is a pleasant park, the Jardin François 1er. In the same area resides the contemporary art museum, **Centre de Création Contemporaine Olivier Debré**, named for one of France's best-known abstract painters from the post-war era, formerly a native of Tours. It includes a café and bookshop. www.cccod.fr

Hours: Open Wednesday through Sunday from 11 am to 6 pm. Saturdays, open until 7 pm. Masks and vaccines are not required.

Admission: 7 €. Under 18, free.

Here is a useful site covering 50 museums of the region: http://musees.regioncentre.fr/les-musees

La Guinguette: An open-air dance hall! Keep going north until you run into the Loire River, then turn right until you reach the Pont Wilson at the top of the Rue Nationale. From mid-May through mid-September, you'll find a river party on the banks of the Loire, with dancing, restaurants, and festivity. It's an annual tradition, called the **guinguette.** It's not the only one in France, but if you're in Tours in summer, you won't want to miss it.

www.touraineloirevalley.co.uk/guinguette-tours-sur-loire/

Find more guinguettes in other locations along the Loire, such as Lulu Parc (www.luluparc.com), Port Avertin (www.ville-saint-avertin.fr), and the town of Savonnières, all nearby Tours. If you visit in winter, check out the winter dance hall at Savonnières.

Just south of the Wilson bridge, you will find the **Musée du Compagnonnage,** a celebration of medieval guilds of manual trades and the finest works of artisans up to the 19th century.

Stonecutters, metalworkers, wood workers, and tanners are just a few trades that had "companions", member artisans who demonstrated superior work to be given the title. Come see the exceptional collections of superior samples of their work, housed in the former abbey of Saint-Julien de Tours, and learn about the fascinating history of guilds in France.

Address: 8 rue Nationale

Hours: Sept. 16 to June 15, open daily (except Tuesday) from 9:00 to 12:30 and 2 to 6 pm. From June 16 to September 15, every day (same hours.) Visits last 1 to 1 ½ hours.

Admission: 6€; Ages up to 26, free.

Botanical Gardens of Tours This is the oldest public garden in the city, dating from 1843, located on the western side of Tours. It consists of 2,000 medicinal and exotic plants, many in greenhouses. It includes theme gardens, phylogenetic gardens, an arboretum, mini-farm, Mediterranean garden, and bog areas.

Address: 334 Boulevard Tonnellé

Hours: in summer, 8 am to 9 pm. September and October, park closes around 7:30 pm. During winter months, park closes at 5:30 pm.

Admission: Free

If you'd like to enjoy the river, there is a peaceful river walk on the western end of the town, where there is a walking path beneath willow trees.

East of Rue Nationale

At this point you have only covered half of the main sites of downtown Tours. Head to the *east side* of Rue Nationale to discover more history and quaint sights with a village feel. Start on the **Rue Colbert**, the main road of the medieval city, which becomes Rue de Commerce as you go west of Rue Nationale. Here you'll see lots of students, but you'll also see 15th and 16th century buildings. Take the Rue de la Scellerie if you want to check out some antique dealers. You'll also see the Grand Theatre, built in 1869. Then at number 39 you'll see the address where Joan of Arc's armor was created in 1429, in preparation for the Siege of Orléans.

Château de Tours Although this region boasts hundreds of castles, the city of Tours has its own overlooking the Loire and protecting the city. Construction began in the 11th century on the remains of Roman baths. In successive centuries the château underwent renovations and repairs. Currently, part of the building is from the 18th century. Inside the castle is a museum depicting the history of Tours, as well as a collection of art by painters such as Miro and Buren, photography, pottery, and sculpture. (Vaccine and mask required.)

Address: 25 Avenue André Malraux

Hours: Open Tuesday through Sunday from 2 pm to 6 pm

Admission: 4€20 for adults, 2€10 for children 12-18.

Eglise Saint Julien de Tours Although this church began as an abbey in the 6th century, it was completed much later in the 13th century in a mixture of Roman and Gothic styles. Between the 6th century and the 20th century it was destroyed or damaged and rebuilt several times. It is one of the oldest churches in France.

Address: 20 Rue Nationale   Open daily.

Eglise Saint Gatien This imposing and ornate cathedral was dedicated to the city's first bishop, St. Gatien. It demonstrates several different styles of architecture from the 13th through the 16th centuries, from Romanesque to Gothic then to Renaissance, though you won't likely notice this as you stand in awe at its ornate beauty.

 Inside are two children's tombs, the last members of the Valois dynasty, the children of Anne of Brittany and King Charles VIII.

Several previous cathedrals stood on the same site but were damaged and rebuilt. The current building dates from 1270, though the work wasn't complete until the 16th-century. That explains the various styles of architecture since Gothic is an earlier style and Renaissance came later. Some of the stained glass is from the 13th-century. A rose window overshadows the 16th-century cathedral organ.

One of the chapels on the grounds was dedicated to Joan of Arc.

Eglise Saint Gatien

Musée de Beaux Arts The 18th century Episcopal palace now houses this impressive art museum, home of paintings, furniture, and objects in a vast collection. Degas, Rubens, Monets, Delacroix . . . such treasures find their home here, around 12,000 objects, though only 1,000 are on display at a time. There should still be plenty to keep you busy there.

Address: 18 Place François Sicard

Hours: Open daily 9:30 to 12:45 and 2:00 pm to 6 pm. Closed Tuesdays.

Admission: 8€ (valid all day); free up to age 26. Students over 26 and people over age 65, 4€. Free the first Sunday of each month.

South of City Hall and Rue Bérangère

Once you descend the Rue Nationale all the way to the Place Jaurès, you'll arrive at the Boulevard Béranger, a wide avenue full of shops, government buildings, and cafés, and lined on either side with mature trees. As you go east past the Place Jaurès, the Rue Bérangère changes names, becoming the Boulevard Heurteloup.

On the Boulevard Béranger side, under shade trees on a wide sidewalk, you'll encounter a burst of color: the weekly **flower market**, an institution every Saturday for the last 100 years.

Weekly Flower Market

The Hotel de Ville is the Tours city hall, created in a similar style to the Hotel de Ville in central Paris.

On the Heurteloup side you will have already discovered the Tours train station (Gare S.N.C.F.), if you arrived by train, as well as the bus station (gare routière.)

Vineyards Near Tours

Château Moncontour This is one of the oldest vineyards in the Loire, featuring Vouvray and Crémant de Loire et Touraine. It includes a wine museum and tasting room. Visits with tasting are free. Museum visits, 5 €. Under 12 free. East of Tours on the north bank of the Loire in Rochecorbon. www.vignobles-feray.fr Open from April to mid-September Monday through Friday from 10 to 6 (closed from 11:30 to 1:30) Open 10 to 12 on Saturdays. In other months, open 10 to 5 (same closure at mid-day) with the same hours on Saturdays.

Cave de Vouvray Go underground and travel a mile of limestone cellars. Enjoy a tasting and learn about winemaking from a special video. The wine shop has many local wines including reds, whites, rosés, and sparkling wines. Open in January and February from 10 am to 12:30 and 2 pm go 6 pm. From March to December open 10 am to 12:30 and 2 pm to 7 pm Monday through Sunday.

Guided tours in English are available from March to December at 11:30 am and 3:30 pm. Adults 4€, children ages 6 to 17, 3€. Under 6, free. Reserve online. Address : 38 Rue de la Vallée Coquette in Vouvray www.cavedevouvray.com

Saint-Roch Between Tours and Vouvray in the town of Rochecorbon you'll find the Grand Caves of Saint-Roch. They have a variety of fine wines from the Loire Valley, including Blanc Foussy, Vouvray, Sancerre, Chinon, and Anjou wines. Guided Tours and tastings are available. 65 Quai de la Loire in Rochecorbon. www.grandescavesstroches.com

Rendez-Vous Dans les Vignes This time, the guided tours take place *in* the vineyards and are followed by tastings of several wines and regional food. Tours range from 25 to 50 €, depending on the type of tour. Sounds fun, doesn't it? www.rdvdanslesvignes.com Other options: learn how to prune grapevines or spend the day sharing in a grape harvest. Meeting place: Vignoble Alain Robert in Charmigny, about 12 miles northeast of Tours, north side of the Loire.

Nearby Exploring

Gadawi Park Aventure : A jungle adventure for the whole family, climbing, running, jumping, and aerial exploits. There are special activities for children as young as 3 years old. Two locations, just minutes from Tours. www.gadawi-park.fr.

Helicopter Ride Fly over the Loire Valley in a helicopter with Airtouraine. Just north of Tours you can board a helicopter or hot air balloon (or blimp!)

Heliport de Belleville in Neuvy le Roi. www.Airtouraine.fr   02.47.24.81.44

Reserve Zoologique de la Haute-Touche. Come see over 1300 animals from 120 species from 5 continents, including tigers and pandas, as well as endangered species, all in their natural habitat. It's like taking a safari while you're still in France! www.zoodelahautetouche.fr/fr in the town of Obterre, France. Phone #: 02.54.02.20.40

Hours: Open every day 10 am to 6 pm April to June. July and August 9 to 7 pm. October to November, Wednesdays, weekends, and holidays open 10 to 5.

Admission: Adults: 14 €; For children 4 to 16 years and students 17-25, 11€. Free for children under 4. Family "Tribal" pass, 2 adults and 2 kids under 12, 44€.

Staying and Eating in Tours

Staying

Luxury

Château Belmont (Clarion Hotel) This château/hotel is on the right bank of the Loire, not far from central Tours. Luxury accommodations, restaurant, spa, and landscaped grounds. www.chateaubelmont.com/fr/

L'Océania l'Univers 5, boulevard Heurteloup. www.oceaniahotels.com/fr/hotel-hotel-oceania-lunivers-tours Very nice four-star hotel, yet affordable, in the center of Tours. Fully renovated in a 150-year-old building.

Budget to Medium-priced

Hôtel Mirabeau 89 bis, boulevard Heurteloup www.hotel-mirabeau.fr This hotel is quite close to the train station, has lovely rooms and a nice breakfast and breakfast room. For email reservations/contact : hotelmirabeau@wanadoo.fr

Appart'Hôtel Néméa Residence Quai Victor, 1 rue Marcel Tribut www.nemea-appart-hotel.com Parking, pool, bike rental, wi-fi available. Each unit has a kitchen, laundry facilities on site. A lot of amenities. Tel. 02.47.70.78.00.

Résidence Leonard de Vinci Appart-hotel, with kitchenette. www.sejours-affaires.com/uk/ 1, place François Truffaut Tel. 02.47.05.19.00.

Appart'Hôtel Odalys This is a chain of apartment-hotels in France. www.odalys-vacation-rental.com

Hôtel Vendome 24 Rue Roger Salengro www.hotelvendome-tours.com email contact and reservations: hotelvendome.tours@numericable.fr.

Small, central hotel in a 19th century building; 5 minutes from the train station. Rooms are individually decorated in unique and retro styles. This is an ecologically oriented hotel, with organic breakfast served each morning.

Eating

La Roche le Roy A fine dining experience for you to taste the traditional flavors of the Loire Valley in an 18th century manor house. Closed Sunday and Monday. 55 Route de Saint Avertin. www.larocheleroy.com/en/the-restaurant/

Le Turon 94 rue Colbert, to the east of Rue Nationale in Vieux (Old) Tours. Open daily for lunch and dinner. Fixed-price menus from 34 € to 39 € featuring local ingredients and recipes in an attractive setting.

La *Deauvalière* 18 rue de la Monnaie, in Vieux Tours. Near the center of the old town, in a 16th-century building. Traditional cuisine from the region, reasonably priced.

Le Vieux Comptoir 10 rue de la Rotisserie (Vieux Tours)   Traditional French food in a cozy atmosphere. Reasonable prices.

Practical Resources in Tours

- Currency Exchange : Normally, you'll be able to use your debit card to withdraw euros € from any ATM. If you need a currency exchange, there is one at the post office: Bureau de Poste, Tours, at 1 Boulevard Béranger OR Welcome Change at 60, rue Bernard Palissy.

- Open Markets: Takes place daily (different locations all over each city) except Monday. See Tourist Bureaus for all addresses and times.

- Bus transportation: Fil Bleu (urban bus) at 9, rue Michelet in Tours.

- Taxis Radio Tours: 1, rue Estienne d'Orves 02.47.20.30.40

- Regional tours by bus:
OuiBus www.ouibus.com   or Flixbus www.flixbus.fr

- Language Courses: Université François Rabelais 3, rue des Tanneurs 02.47.36.66.00

Excursions and Package Tours

You can get a lot of information and scheduling at the Tourist Bureau in Tours, but here are some companies you can check out online before you go. **Many of these will cover the entire Loire Valley.** All of them will do day trips and some do multi-day trips or packages. You can find individual visits if you are creating your own trip. Read carefully what each one offers to be sure what they include. Some are mainly for transportation but for lunch and château admission, you are on your own. Others will include everything, plus commentary.

1. **Acco Dispo Excursions**
    (06.82.00.64.51) www.accodispo-tours.com/tours.html Departures from either Tours or Amboise.

2. **Loire Valley à La Carte**
    (07.81.61.19.58) A la carte or packages for seeing the Loire Valley.
    http://www.loirevalleyalacarte.com/

3. **Loire Valley Sightseeing Tours**
    (custom private tours) (09.73.68.74.53)

4. **Loire Valley Tours** (02. 47.79.40.20) Tours for vineyards, biking, castles, etc. from 1 to 5 days. www.loire-valley-tours.com/en/

5. **A la Française** Small group half or full-day tours departing from Tours, Amboise, or Paris. www.alafrancaise.fr/en/loire-valley/

6. **Touraine Evasion** (06.07.39.13.31) Châteaux excursions from Tours or Amboise. Half (morning or afternoon) or full day tours. www.tourevasion.com/prog_en.htm

7. **Val de Loire Travel** (07.86.46.94.07) Castle or wine tours, packages or customizable. www.valdeloire-travel.com/en/

Northeast Loire Valley

For your visit to the Loire Valley, you will surely want to see the northeast section. Not only is there is a lot to see and do there, but this is the place to find some of the most renowned and sumptuous châteaux in the world. For example, think of Chambord, a castle legendary in size, the largest in the Loire Valley. The cities of Amboise and Blois will enchant you as well and fill your days with sights and activities.

The two main cities in this area you'll want to visit are *Amboise* and *Blois*, with other towns and châteaux located close by. If you're eager to see châteaux, you won't be disappointed. You could use Amboise as a base for your entire stay in this area or divide your time between Amboise and Blois.

There are three main châteaux to see in and around Amboise (Amboise, Clos Lucé, and Chaumont), and 3 more in and around Blois (Blois, Cheverny, and Chambord.) Short summaries of each château on the following pages and on page 160 will help you decide where you want to go. You can research and organize your own trip or enlist the help of a tour company for tours lasting anywhere between a half day and several days. For Tour companies see pages 45-46.

Amboise

You can get to Amboise by TGV train in just over an hour. There are between 12 and 16 trains per day from Paris (either Montparnasse or Austerlitz stations) that can take you there. If you have begun your travels in Tours, you can get to Amboise from Tours in about 30 minutes by train or car.

When you get off the train at the Gare (train station) you'll be on the north bank of the Loire, though most of the city is on the south bank. It's a short walk to cross the river by a scenic sidewalk. If you're driving, you'll also want to aim for the southern bank of the Loire to access the town. As you cross the bridge, either on foot or by car, you won't have trouble finding the town, since you'll see the château well before you get there.

The Tourist Bureau for Amboise is located across from the river at Quai du General de Gaulle. www.amboise-valdeloire.com

History

The city of Amboise goes way back to the 6th century and has many noteworthy moments throughout its history. It's first inhabitants were the Turones, a Celtic people, the same group that first settled in Tours.

From the 15th to the 17th centuries, Amboise was the center of the French monarchy, although today there are fewer than 15,000 residents. (The tourist scene, however, is another story!) Charles VIII, from the House of Valois, lived there in the 15th century with his wife, Anne of Brittany. His marriage to her brought the region of Brittany into France. (Read more of their amazing true story of intrigue and tragedy on page 87.)

A later event worth noting involved another French king, François I (Francis, in English.) François was a great fan of all things Italian during the Italian Renaissance. Hoping to bring some Italian artistic flavor to France, he invited Leonardo da Vinci to Amboise to live. The king gave Leonardo a slightly smaller château to live in, called Clos Lucé, and a generous allowance. Da Vinci died in Amboise three years later and is buried in the chapel on the grounds of the Amboise château. (Read more about the Châteaux of Amboise and Clos Lucé a bit later ...)

Seeing and Doing

The Royal Château of Amboise has remnants going back to the 4th century when trenches were dug to defend nearby residents. It became a royal residence in the 15th century. At that time, Louis XI lived there with his wife Charlotte de Savoie. Their son was Charles VIII. The year following Charles' marriage to Anne of Brittany, he did extensive building on the château where he'd spent his childhood, completing the Saint Hubert Chapel in the Gothic style as well as the medieval Lodge. Construction continued for several years afterward, with Gothic and Italian influences, until his accidental death at a young age. Later kings continued building and more Renaissance architectural styles emerged over time.

Chateau and town of Amboise

Inside the St. Hubert Chapel on the grounds of the Château, in addition to a lovely, airy space with ornately carved walls and buttresses, you'll see the burial plaque for Leonardo da Vinci, who died in 1519.

Over the subsequent centuries the Château was neglected, used as a prison, inhabited by passing sovereigns, and purchased by other nobles who restored it in varying degrees. Quite a bit of the present castle is not original and a few of the rooms are not furnished, but the end result is still worth a visit.

From the roof of the château's Tour des Minimes and the Tour Hurtault you can look out over the Loire. The cavalier ramp is a tower with a circular ramp inside where horses could climb to the upper terraces of the structure. The gardens are reminiscent of Italian terraces and contain a statue of Leonardo da Vinci.

Hours: Open daily from 9 am to 6:30 pm; Guided tours are available in French and audio guides are available in English.

Admission: Adults, 13.50€. Students 11.60€, Children 9€20. Under age 7, free.

Clos Lucé The château where Leonardo spent his last 3 years of life bears many signs of his genius and creativity. You can walk from the Château d'Amboise to Clos Lucé in only a few minutes. The original name of the castle was Château de Cloux, built in 1471 on top of 12th century foundations. The main building surrounds an octagonal tower with a spiral stairway. It was purchased by Charles VIII and inhabited over the next centuries by several royals in the family. Leonardo da Vinci, however, was the best-known resident. When he accepted King François' invitation, he brought with him the Mona Lisa, and that is how the painting made its way to France.

Leonardo was appointed the "first painter, architect, and engineer" of the king. He was given a generous salary and complete freedom to create, invent, and entertain the king and the king's friends in lavish parties. Inside the château as well as on the landscaped grounds outside, you'll find his varied creations, from the first "car" to the first "helicopter", his workshop, and numerous paintings and experiments in engineering, including 20 working mobile models. In addition, there are rooms furnished according to the period, portraits, and frescoes.

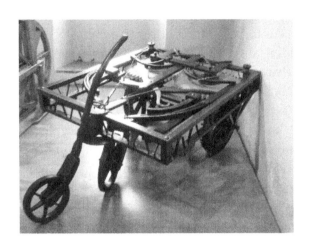
Leonardo Da Vinci's "Car"

<u>Hours</u>: January open from 10 am to 6 pm. February through June and September through October, open from 9 am to 7 pm. July and August open from 9 am to 8 pm. November and December, open from 9 am to 6 pm.

<u>Admission</u>: Adults, 18€, children 7 to 18 years and students, 12€50, Tickets are available online or at the château. Family passes are available.
www.vinci-closluce.com/en/place-presentation

Chaumont This château fulfills one's imagination of what a castle should look like, with pointed slate roofs and round towers on each corner. You'll picture medieval knights, fairy tales, the prince, and

54

the princess. Established in the 10th century, the appearance looks newer. And it is, because the château was destroyed and rebuilt in the 15th century, adding some Italian Renaissance influences. Most of the owners were nobility, not monarchs, until it was purchased in 1560 by Catherine de Medici. She lived there while her husband's mistress, Diane de Poitiers, lived at Chenonceau. When Catherine's husband, Henri II, died, Catherine ousted Diane from Chenonceau, but allowed her to live in Chaumont instead. Catherine then moved into Chenonceau herself and enlarged it. (Read about Chenonceau in the Southeast, page 90.)

Getting there: Chaumont is located just a few miles east of Amboise, about a mile past a small town called Onzain. If you are coming by car, look for the town Chaumont-sur-Loire on departmental roads D-952 and D751. If you come by autoroute, the French highway, the château is accessible by the A10 or A85.

Hours: Open all year. January open 10 am to 5:30 pm. February and March open from 10 am to 6 pm. April 1-20, open 10 to 7. Then through the end of August, open from 10 am to 8 pm. September, open from 10 am to 7:30 pm. October 1-29, open 10 am to 7 pm. October 30 to November 6, open from 10 am to 6 pm. November 7 to December 31, open from 10 am to 5:30 pm. I think that's everything...

Admission: April 21 to October 31, Adult, 19€, child age 6 to 11, 6€. Ages 12 to 18, 12 €. Children under 6, free. Low season, Adults 14€, children 4€. Tickets available online. www.domaine-chaumont.fr/en

A lesser-known but nonetheless impressive château in the region is the **Château de Gué-Péan**, just a few miles southeast of Amboise and east of Chenonceau in the town of Monthou-sur-Cher.

At Gué-Péan, built in the 14th and 15th centuries, the interior is cozier than some others, thanks to the wood paneling and tapestries, and more recent furnishings in the styles of Louis XV and XVI. It was used as a hunting lodge by the many kings and nobles who stayed there.

Hours: At the time of this writing, the chateau is temporarily closed. Reopens July 2022. Previous opening times: Open mid-July to late August from 10:30 to 12:30 and 2 pm to 6:30 pm. Check the website as open dates will vary year to year. https://www.experienceloire.com/gue-pean.htm

Admission: Adults 6.50, children 9 to 12, 5 €. Under 9, free.

Pagoda of Chanteloup The Chanteloup Château from the 18th century was once compared to the Château of Versailles in opulence, but sadly, the château was destroyed in 1823. What remains is the surrounding land and something surprising . . . a pagoda. It was built in 1775 by the Duke of Choiseul to honor the friends who stood by him following his expulsion from Louis XV's court. Climb 149 steps to the top and get great views of the surrounding countryside. It is situated next to a lake and Chinese gardens in a 35-acre park. The Pagoda is about 2 miles from Amboise. www.pagode-chanteloup.com

Hours: Open March 18 to May 31, open 10 am to 6 pm. June 1 to August 31, open 10 to 7. September, 10 am to 6 pm. During October, 2 pm to 6 pm. November, 2 pm to 5 pm.

Admission: 10€50 for adults, children ages 7 to 18, 8€, and students 9€50. Family passes available. Boat rides 5 €.

Parc Mini Châteaux de la Loire If you'd like an overview of 41 Loire Valley Châteaux all in one day, visit the Parc Mini Château de la Loire, a park like none other you've seen. As you stroll around, you'll view at 1:25 scale, mini replicas of some of the most beautiful châteaux of the Loire Valley, including Chambord, Blois, Villandry, and Saumur. You can order tickets online or on site. Combination tickets with the Grand Aquarium de Touraine (page 61) are also available.

Getting there: Address is Boulevard St. Denis Hors in Amboise.

Hours: April to July 8, open from 10 am to 6:30 pm. July 9 to September 4, open from 9:30 to 7 pm. In September open from 10:30 to 6 pm. For other months, consult the website.
https://www.parcminichateaux.com/calendrier-visite-amboise-touraine

Admission: Adults and children over age 18 cost 14€50. Children ages 4 to 12, 10€50.

Vineyards in and near Amboise

Here are several addresses where you can visit vineyards and taste a variety of Loire Valley wines, learning about them and perhaps bringing a bottle home with you!

Caves Duhard (Cave Ambacia) 6 rue du Rocher des Violettes, Amboise. Tel. 02 47 57 20 77
Bistro open daily 10 am to 8 pm. Tours can be reserved in advance. contact@caves-ambacia.fr.

Closerie de Chanteloup, 460, Route de St-Martin-le-Beau, Amboise. Wine from organic farming, and home-made beer as well!

Plou et Fils in the nearby town of Chargé, to the east of Amboise. This family has made wine since 1508! Located at 26, rue du General du Gaulle in Chargé.

The following three vineyards are in the town of Limeray, north of Amboise across the Loire River.

Domaine Dutertre Wine caves and museum. A family winery for 5 generations. Place du Tertre, 20-21, rue d'Enfer. Open Monday to Saturday 9 am to 12:30pm, 2 to 6 pm. Tel. 02.47.30.10.69.

Domaine des Bessons Underground wine caves, tastings. 113 Rue de Blois, Limeray. Tel. 02.47.30.90.10.

Domaine Mesliand is another organic farm, family-made for four generations. Located 6, rue de Blois in Limeray.

For a change, visit *La Distillerie Fraise-Or*, between the towns of Chenonceaux and Montrichard at 441400 Chissay en Touraine. Liqueurs and Eaux de Vie from the Loire region.

Open daily between Easter and late September, 9 am to 11:30 and 2 pm to 6 pm. Tel. 02.54.32.32.05.

Nearby Exploring

Valmer Gardens Close to Amboise (10 minutes) is the Château de Valmer, an Italian Renaissance château with five centuries of history. There are 13 acres of gardens on 8 terraces and 150 acres of historical forest. The vineyard produces Vouvray and rosé wines, which you can taste for free.

Getting there: Take the D31 toward Autrèche then D55 and D5 toward Reugny. Follow the D46 toward Chançay.

Hours: Open for visits April 29 to October 2 from 2 pm to 8 pm Wednesday through Sunday. Otherwise, open for wine sales and special events. Garden tours by appointment.
https://www.chateaudevalmer.com/en/

Admission: 10€. Children 10 to 18, 7€.

Musée du Cuir et de la Tannerie (Museum of Leather) This unusual museum is a short drive north of Amboise. In the 19th century there were many shoe factories and tanneries in the area. This museum resides in an old tannery and shows the methods and history of leatherworking.

Address: 105 ter, rue de la République in the town of Chateau-Renault. Workshops for children (7 and older) and adults are available. After this 2-hour workshop you'll have a project to take with you. Cost, 10 €. Reservations: Tel. 01.47.56.03.59. Open May 1 to September 30 from 2 pm to 6 pm. Closed Mondays. Tours 2:30 pm and 4:30 pm.

Admission: Adults, 5€, students 2€50. Under 10, free.

Grand Aquarium de Touraine This is the largest fresh-water aquarium in France, with 63 individual aquariums containing 2 million liters of water. Exhibits on the Loire River history, a shark tunnel, and much more.

Getting there By car, it is a 5-minute drive from Amboise and 20 minutes from Tours in the town of Lussault-sur-Loire. There is also a bus from Amboise. Go toward the town of Montlouis and descend at the Aquarium stop.

Hours: Open daily from 10:00 am to 6:30 pm from April through June. July and August, open until 7 pm. Check website for winter hours.

Admission: Adults, 14€50. Children ages 4 to 12, 10€50 and ages 13 to 17, 12€50. You can buy tickets online or on site. A combination ticket with the nearby Mini-Château Park or a family pass is also available.

Art Museum Musée-Hôtel Morin, also called Musée de l'Hôtel de Ville. In the 16th century private home of Pierre Morin, treasurer to King Louis XII, you'll find several rooms of works of art, as well as a few municipal buildings, including those hosting wedding ceremonies.

Getting there: Rue Francois 1er, Amboise

Hours: Open daily (closed Tuesday) between June 15 and September 16 from 10 am to 12:30 and from 2 to 6 pm.

Admission: Free

Pottery Gallery Three minutes from Amboise is a pottery workshop where you can either browse finished pieces or take a class. Wheel Classes of 60 or 90 minutes available for children or adults. 17 rue Julia Daudet in the nearby town of Chargé. Www.poterieenfolie.com .

Biking Touring by bike around the town of Amboise and the quiet streets will give you a different perspective. Here are a couple of bike rental companies you can check out while you are there.

Maps available at the Tourist Bureau can lead you from one château to another.

Locacycle: Open every day 9 am to 7 pm. Free accessories, sliding scale after third day. http://www.locacycle-amboise.fr/. 2 Rue Jean-Jacques Rousseau, Amboise.

Detours de Loire Bike rentals by hour, half-day, day, week or month. 02.47.30.00.55. Avenue du General de Gaulle.

Hot Air Ballooning
Ballooning has become popular in the Loire Valley and you can imagine why. Picture yourself sailing silently over majestic châteaux in a memorable balloon ride. Here are a few companies you can survey for information about routes, rides, prices, and other conditions. (Note: Hot air balloon in French is a *Montgolfière*.)

- Au Gré des Vents www.au-gre-des-vents.fr
- Balloon Revolution
  www.balloonrevolution.com
- Touraine Montgolfière
  www.touraine-montgolfiere.fr
- Aerocom Montgolfières www.aerocom.fr
- France Montgolfières
  www.franceballoons.com/

63

Train tours Take a 40-minute sight-seeing tour by train around the city of Amboise with commentary on its history and secrets. Train tours leave from the Office of Tourism of Amboise and finish up at the Château Clos Lucé (Da Vinci's castle.)

Mushroom Farm Caves des Roches. Go deep underground to a unique "city" on seven levels carved out of limestone. Learn about mushroom cultivation and taste a few if you like! This unique mushroom farm produces 100 tons of mushrooms per year! www.le-champignon.c6om

Getting there: 40 route des Roches in the town of Bourré, which is just north of the town of Montrichard (southeast of Amboise close to Chenonceaux.)

Hours: Open daily from April to mid-November. Guided visits are an hour long and take place at 10 am, 11 am, at 2 pm, 3pm, 4 pm, and 5 pm in French.

Admission: Adults and children over 14 years, 12€. Children under 16, 7€50.

Spa: Centre de Bien-Etre (Center for Well-Being) in Amboise. 11, Allee du Sergent Turpin in Amboise. (Temporarily closed due to Covid. Call for updates) 02.47.57.08.52

Staying and Eating in Amboise

Staying

Le Domaine des Thomeaux is a luxury hotel with a spa and restaurant. Or you could just come and enjoy the spa, your choice. 12 rue des Thomeaux, in the town of Mosnes, just east of Amboise. www.domainedesthomeaux.fr/

Le Clos d'Amboise A 4-star hotel right in Amboise resides in a 17th century manor that was renovated in 2011. Luxurious rooms and an elegant restaurant will enable you to stay in style during your time in the Loire. Five minutes from the château. 27 rue Rabelais in Amboise. www.leclosdamboise.com

La Brèche A nice two-star hotel right near the Amboise train station, perfectly located if you are arriving by train. 26, rue Jules Ferry. Simple but neat, with a lovely breakfast available at extra cost. www.labreche-amboise.com

Eating

L'Epicerie Traditional French cuisine in a half-timbered 14th century building, the oldest one in

Amboise. Cozy décor, with a fixed-price menu between 15 and 31 €. Located at the foot of the château, 46 Place Michel Debré.

Le Lion d'Or For an upscale dining experience (but still affordable) dine in this 18th century house turned restaurant with three different dining rooms of different styles, contemporary, cozy, and elegant. 17 Quai Charles Guinot.

Restaurant Anne de Bretagne This restaurant at the foot of the Amboise chateau has good home cooking, crêpes, and is reasonably priced for lunch or dinner. Located at 1 Montée de l'Emir Abdel Kader. They also have a terrace.

La Cave aux Fouées For a unique dining experience, try a "troglodyte" cave restaurant, where the specialty is homemade "fouées", like pitas, cooked on site in brick ovens. Traditional French cuisine "a l'ancienne", or as they used to do, and Saturday night dancing to 80s tunes. 476, quai des Violettes in Amboise. 02.47.30.56.80. For more info, check out: www.lacaveauxfouees.com

Lounge B Piano Bar Discover wines and spirits of the Loire Valley while listening to music and munching on tapas. 12, Quai Charles Guinot (opposite the bridge.)

Specialty Stores

Galland If you want to be sure to taste some regional specialties and prefer to buy them in a food boutique (épicerie), take a stroll through Galland, inside an 18th century building. There are over 1500 products including wine, paté, champagne, macarons, candies, jams, condiments, and a whole array of French regional specialties. For souvenirs, gifts, and gourmet snacking! 27 rue National in Amboise.

Organic Food Store (called Amboise Alimentation Biologique et Produits Ecologiques) This is the largest organic food store between Tours and Blois, with a vast variety of products. Located at 46 rue Victor Hugo in Amboise. Open Tuesday through Sunday 9:30 am to 1 pm, 2:30 to 7 pm.

Blois

Blois (pronounced Blwah) is an historic château city perched alongside the right, or north bank of the Loire River. It's also central enough to the other must-see châteaux to be a good home base or a second stop following Amboise.

A first step is to head for the *centre-ville*, or city center. If you are driving, just follow signs to centre-ville and Château. Both will be clearly marked. There is underground parking available near the château.

The Tourist Bureau is across from the château, so you can't miss it. They can give you information about things to see in the town as well as in the surrounding region. Be sure to ask for the walking tour map of the town itself. It will orient you as well as take you to sites you might not otherwise know about.

There are also guided visits to Old Blois. Ask about these at the Tourist Information Bureau. A free smartphone app is available for you to discover the natural and architectural heritage of Blois for 100 locations around the city. Access these through the App Store and Google Play.

The city of Blois boasts 65 monuments and 1000 years of history.

History

By the middle of the 10th century Blois was occupied by the Counts of Blois, vassals of the King of France. There had been a fortress in the 13th century and the counts rebuilt it several times. The current château is a patchwork from history, with only a few chunks of the original ramparts remaining.

In the 14th century, the château was sold to the royal family to the prince of Orléans, son of Charles V. This put Blois "on the map", so to speak, in terms of royal importance and cultural development. Charles V's son lived there for over two decades and brought in many scholars and poets. Then his grandson, Louis XII, became king. He took the place of his cousin, Charles VIII on the throne, after the latter's untimely death. Louis then married Charles VIII's widow, Anne de Bretagne. Blois was like the second capital of France at the time, after Paris.

Under Louis' reign and that of his successor, François (Francis) I, the town grew and prospered. François married Anne's daughter, Claude. After her death he left the Blois castle and took up his residence in Amboise. (He was the king who invited Leonardo da Vinci to France.) He was also very involved in many castle building projects: Amboise, Blois, Chambord, Fontainebleau, and even the Louvre in Paris, which used to be a castle.

Seeing and Doing in Blois

Old Town This is a great place to start your visit in Blois, seeing the Renaissance and medieval features of the streets and town squares. Look for more medieval homes and buildings on the Rue du Puits-Chatel and Rue Pierre de Blois.

Each Wednesday evening from mid-July to mid-August at 8 pm you can enjoy street theatre where burlesque-style actors illustrate part of the city's history. It's free and takes place at the Place du Château.

Château Royal de Blois The Château is a centerpiece of the town of Blois, even though there is a lot more to see and do. You could start your visit here then circle outward to take in the other sights and energy of the town. It's stunning inside and outside, and worth a visit.

For many centuries the Château Royal was the favored residence of the counts of Blois, except for a lengthy period of history when King Louis XII and François I, and 5 other kings (and 7 queens), made it their home. François I later moved to Amboise and eventually the monarchy was moved to Paris.

Château of Blois

The château is endowed with four different architectural styles since it was embellished over four centuries by various monarchs. One notable feature is an exterior staircase facing the inner courtyard in an ornate Renaissance design on the wing known as François (Francis) I's wing. You can see the whole château in miniature at the nearby Parc Mini Châteaux de la Loire (see page 57). This is an especially good way to get an overview of its four architectural styles and wings.

Inside the château there are 30 furnished rooms, and a fine art museum. You can do a self-guided tour with an audioguide available in 8 languages for 3€ extra. There are quite a few special seasonal activities and events throughout the year (See below for more details about events.)

A few minutes' walk from the château, you'll find Les Jardins du Roy, a contemporary garden inspired by previous ones which were part of the castle but later parceled out. Though not original, it offers pools, fountains, and a beautiful view of the city and château. The remaining vestiges of the original garden are the Orangerie and the Pavillon Anne de Bretagne (3 avenue Jean-Laigret). This was a place where Anne could escape to a smaller, simpler space and enjoy the 5 fireplaces and, perhaps, mourn her deceased children. The Pavillon is free to visit and open from March to late December from 2 pm to 6 pm Wednesday through Saturday. Entrance to Les Jardins du Roy is also free.

Special Events at the Château

Special art exhibits take place for limited time periods.

On May 21 for a national festival called the *Nuit des Musées* (night of the museums) enjoy extended hours and special programs and shows.

From July 14 to late August there are Renaissance dances every Friday and Saturday.

From early April to late September enjoy a sound and light show projected on the façade of the castle on the courtyard side. Showings in April, May, and September are at 10 pm. Showings in June, July, and August at 10:30 pm.

Also, in summer is a fencing show, featuring the medieval style of fencing, recapturing the duels of the Middle Ages in a humorous way.

Lastly, at Christmas there are special programs that take place at the Château. See the castle website for full details or visit the Tourism Bureau for a full description and brochures.

Getting there: The Château Royal sits along the left bank of the Loire at the Place du Château. If you are traveling by car, follow signs to the château.

Hours: The château is open all year, except January 1 and December 25. From January 2 to March 31 and from November 7 to December 31, open 10 am to 5 pm. April 1 to June 30 and September 1 to November 1, open 9 am to 6:30 pm. July 1 to August 31, open 9 am to 7 pm.

Admission: Adults, 13€, students 10€, children ages 6 to 17, 6€50. Children under 6, free. Guided tours, audio guides, and combination tickets (sound and light show, house of magic, Doute Foundation Art museum, visit of Old Blois) are available. See their website for details. www.chateaudeblois.fr/ Combination tickets with other castles and sites in the city are also available. For all details see www.bloischambord.com

Cathédrale de Saint Louis de Blois 17th century cathedral whose bell tower is lit up at night. It demonstrates late Gothic architecture, though there are some medieval features as well. Behind it is the gardens, the Jardins de l'Evêché with rose gardens and a view of the Valley.

Eglise de Saint Nicolas on Rue St-Laumer. This was the church associated with a monastery from the 12th century. It was an important place of pilgrimage and contains several relics.

Maison de la BD (House of Comics, or Bandes dessinées.) Open since 2015, this comics headquarters will entertain big and small fans of comics as well as art in general. Exhibits and conferences are held throughout the year. Classes are available as well, if you are staying in Blois for a while. Located at 3 rue des Jacobins. Open 9:30 am to 12 pm and 2 pm to 5:30 pm.

Maison des Acrobates A 15th century half-timbered house named for the acrobats carved on the front façade. It's worth a look to observe the interesting figures on the façade. Located at 3 and 3bis (and a half) Place Saint Louis.

Maison de la Magie House of Magic, featuring magician Robert Houdin, after whom Houdini named himself. A museum like no other, come see optical illusions (including dragons emerging from windows) and games, learn the history of magic, and discover the work of Robert Houdin, a famous French magician. Five floors will entertain you and your children, especially the interactive "Hallucinoscope".

Getting there: 1 Place du Château

Hours: Open from April 1 to August 31 daily from 10 am to 12:30 pm and 2 pm to 6:30 pm. From mid-October to early November, open 2 pm to 6:30 daily. Ticket booth closes 30 minutes before closing.

Admission: Adults 10€, children ages 6 to 17, 6€50. Combination tickets available with Château. (See previous listing for the Château.)

Doute Foundation A contemporary art museum, but unusual in its approach, because it's an interactive, artistic space. Come discover over 300 works by 50 artists with plaques and thought questions posed throughout by artist "Ben". Café "Le Fluxus" is on site for your refreshments.

Getting there: 14 rue de la Paix. Tel 02.54.55.37.40 www.fondationdudoute.fr

<u>Hours</u>: Currently closed until <u>July 2022</u> for renovations. From July 2 to August 28 open from 2 pm to 6:30 pm daily, Tuesday to Sunday. From August 31 to November open Wednesday through Sunday from 2 pm to 6:30 pm. November 12 to December 18, open Friday to Sunday, 2 to 6:30 pm. Closed January 1 to February 7 and December 24 to 31.

<u>Admission</u>: Adults, 7€50. Children ages 6 to 17, 3€50. Students, 5€50. Possibility of combined tickets with Château Royal. See Château listing above for information.

Nearby Exploring

Ancient tools and folk-art museum (Musée d'Outils Anciens et d'Art Populaire) This museum features over 1,000 tools from the 19th and 20th centuries. They reflect the lives and times of rural artisans of that epoch. Located at 18, rue du Vieux Porche in the nearby town of Les Montils, due south of Blois.

Troglodyte Villages A Troglodyte is a modern cave-dweller. Throughout the Loire Valley, where there is an abundance of limestone caves and cliffs, there are troglodyte homes, dwellings that have been carved into the cliff. Only the front façade of the

house is visible. In the past, whole villages have been underground, and you can see some of them today. One of these is the **Village of Trôo**. This village is on three different levels. The bottom level is the oldest, dating to medieval times. There are pathways, streets, even a church and a well. Many other troglodyte homes are scattered through this area, some inhabited. You can download a map of the town in English here
https://trootourisme.jimdo.com/

<u>Getting there</u>: 39 rue August Arnaud, 41800 Trôo. More info: Tel. 02.54.72.87.50. Near Blois.

<u>Hours</u>: Open all year from 10 to 12 and 2 to 4 pm.

Troglodyte House in a Cliff

<u>Admission</u>: Adults 7€. Children, 4€ Guided tours in French, info sheets in other languages. For info about visits on their site, Visits and Sites tab.

Another troglodyte village that is inhabited is in the town of Bourré, about a half hour drive south of Blois, and east of Chenonceaux. It is called *La Magnanerie* (which means a place that produces silk, because silk production was done in the village.) Guided visits are 60-75 minutes long and your guide lives in the village. Though the visit is in French, you'll have a summary in English and 4 other languages.

<u>Getting there</u>: 4, Chemin de la Croix Bardin, 41400 Bourré Tel. 02.54.75.50.79

<u>Hours of visits</u> : February 5 to March 6 at 11:30 am and 2:30 pm. From April 9 to July 15, at 11:30 am, 2:30 pm, and 4:30 pm. From July 16 to August 28, visits at 11:30, 2:30, 3:30, 4:30 and 5:30. From August 29 to September 29, and also from October 22 to November 6. Call to book. Covid pass required. Closed on Tuesdays.

<u>Admission</u>: Adults 9€; children age 6 to 12, 5€, ages 13 to 17 are 7 €. Under 6, free.

A third troglodyte village can be found in the town of **Rochemenier,** to the west of Amboise. https://www.experienceloire.com/trogs.htm

Here's an original lodging option, a troglodyte hotel! Here is one: Cote Sud B & B A top-rated bed and breakfast in a 17th century house in the Trôo village.

Château de Chambord This is one of the best-known châteaux in the Loire Valley, in particular, for its size. It is the largest in France, with over 400 rooms (and a fireplace in almost all of them) and sits like a mountain on a flat piece of land. There aren't many trees, but next to it lies a body of water that reflects its grandeur. The Château has a large formal garden. One can easily recognize the building from a distance for its many rounded towers all along the outside, almost making it look like a whipped confection!

It is not far from Blois, which makes for a nice daytrip from there. The Renaissance château was built by François I, though the land came into royal ownership before that, when Louis XII became king. It was built as a country residence and hunting reserve and required 1800 men to build it. It wasn't François' primary residence, however, which he divided between Amboise and Blois. In fact, he hardly spent time there at all, and after his death, it sat empty for almost 100 years.

Chateau de Chambord

Inside there is a double spiral staircase, which may have been inspired by one designed by Leonardo da Vinci, but never completed prior to his death.

All around the château is a park with as large a surface area as the city of Paris! In fact, it is the largest walled park in France. There are miles of hidden paths and lovely landscapes. You can even explore these by horseback or in a 4-wheeler vehicle (with a private nature guide), at extra cost. The formal French gardens, which were destroyed during the World Wars, were fully restored in 2017, and cover 16 acres. These are included in the château admission ticket.

Other château grounds activities include boat rental, electric cars, and carriage rides. During the year there are special events as well, such as exhibits and lectures by a well-known writer the last Sunday of each month. June 21 is the Music Festival (throughout France, and Chambord will not be left out!) There are other concerts as well, and the first half of July is the Chambord Festival. At Christmas, special activities and decorations will celebrate the holidays and ring in the New Year. For prices and other info: www.chambord.org

If you'd like to stay in a cottage just at the gates of the château, email for info: gites-chambord@chambord.org .

Getting there: The Chambord castle is about a 25-minute drive from Blois on Route N17 and about an hour from Tours in the town of Chambord.

Hours: Open daily. January 2 to March 25, and October 31 to December 16, open from 9 am to 5 pm. From March 26 to October 30, and from December 17 to December 31, open 9 am to 6 pm. Gardens close 30 minutes prior to château closing.

Admission: Château and gardens, Adults, 14.50 €. Children under 18, free. Ages 18 to 25, 12 €. E.U. residents to age 25, free. Extra cost for the use of a *Histopad*, which is an interactive tablet that guides you through the château, explains the history, and gives 3D views in virtual reality of the way it was then. Includes over an hour of commentary on the history and architecture of the château. 6€50 extra or 17€ for a "family pack", or 3 tablets. Guided visits in English are available from July to September at 11:15 am daily for 5€ extra. Parking: 4€ per day for cars. 11€ for campers valid 24 hours (though no camping allowed.) Parking for bikes is free.

Château de Cheverny This was the first private château that became a public tourist site in 1922. It was in the same family for six centuries, and the current owners still live in one of the wings. It is one of the better-furnished châteaux of the Loire Valley, and the furnishings, many dating back to the Louis XIII period, are worth seeing. And don't overlook the Hall of Trophies, where you'll see 2,000 pairs of antlers and an impressive stained-glass window depicting the estate.

There are two beautiful gardens, one with over a thousand tulip bulbs (one source says 120,000!), whose gorgeous colors are displayed each April (usually, though this depends on the weather.)

One of the notable features of this château is . . . dogs! Dog-lovers will enjoy the daily feeding ritual of over 100 English Foxhounds and French Poitevin. They are a part of the Cheverny hunt, which has taken place for the last 150 years. Dog feeding is open to the public and takes place at 11:30 am year-round. (Exception: Tuesday, Saturdays, Sundays, and holidays between September 15 and March 31.) Close to the chateau are historic apartments where you can stay. See the website for details.3Also, in the park you can enjoy electric cars and boat rides from April to November. Throughout the year there are special events, such as the Miss France pageant in June, a plant festival in late March, visits to see the tulips in bloom, in April.

Chateau de Cheverny

In addition, there are Christmas programs, fireworks, an auto rally, and a jazz festival June 30 and July 1.

The château was used as a prototype castle for Moulinsart, the setting of beloved French cartoon characters such as Tintin, Captain Haddock, and Tournesol, demonstrated by exhibits inside the château. Parking is free.

Getting there: The château is a short drive from Blois, from Chambord and from Chenonceau in the town of Cheverny. Route N152.

Hours: Open all year, including Christmas, New Years and May 1. From January 1 to March 31 and from October 1 to December 31, open from 10 am to 5 pm. From April 1 to September 30 open from 10 am to 6pm.

Admission: For the château and gardens, Adults 13€50, children ages 7 to 14 and students up to age 25, 9€. Under age 7, free. For the château, gardens, and exposition of Moulinsart and Tintin (see previous), Adults 17€, children ages 7 to 14 and students to age 25, costs 13€. Château, gardens, boat ride and electric cars, Adults 18€, children ages 7 to 14 and students up to age 25, 13.50 €. Children under 7, free. For all four activities (château, gardens, Tintin expo, and boat/car), Adults 22 €, children ages 7 to 14 and students to 25 years, 17€50, and children under 7, 4€.

In other words, you could easily spend the whole day, maybe two, at the Château de Cheverny!

Staying and Eating in and around Blois

Château du Breuil (hotel-château) Here is another château in Cheverny . . . but you can *stay* at this one since it is a four-star hotel on the grounds of the Château de Cheverny. An 18th-century castle that has been fully suited to guests, Château du Breuil includes a swimming pool, dining room, and bikes to borrow so that you can explore the lush surroundings. 39 rooms and suites are available. 23, routes de Fougères, Cheverny. Info@chateau-hotel-du-breuil.com. www.chateau-hotel-du-breuil.com

Le Monarque Hotel et Restaurant This clean and central three-star hotel is a good choice for the budget traveler, and it's quite close to the château. Double rooms with bathroom available for around 75€ to 90€, depending on the season. 61, rue Porte Chartraine, Blois. The establishment has received the label Logis de France, a French network of quality lodgings. www.hotel-lemonarque.com/fr

Eating

Le Castelet 40 rue Saint Lubin, Blois. Traditional French cuisine served in a 16th century manor house in Old Blois. The menu features locally sourced ingredients in three choices: A main course with either appetizer or dessert for 29 €, all three for

35€50, or all three plus a cheese plate for 40€50. Vegetarian or pescatarian meals included for 30€.

Assa 189 Quai Ulyssé-Besnard, Blois. Prix fixe meals with several courses each from 64 to 124€ (some are for two main courses.) A la carte pricing is around 44€ for a main course. You can dine overlooking the river for a peaceful break from your travels. Vegetarian and vegan options are available.

Au Rendez-Vous des Pêcheurs 27 Rue du Foix, Blois. Newly renovated. Menu fixe prices range from 18€ to 65€. Located in the center of Blois near the river, this seafood restaurant is as elegant as its menu.

All of the above restaurants are recommended or starred by Michelin.

Anne de Bretagne

As you learn about the history of the châteaux of the Loire Valley, this fascinating woman keeps showing up. Her life story makes a most interesting soap opera!

Born in 1477, Anne was raised in Nantes during a time when Brittany wasn't yet part of France. Her father, Francis II, was the Duke of Brittany. After his death, she became the duchess at the age of eleven, though this was contingent on her marriage. She was betrothed a number of times for political reasons, but each betrothal fell through. She finally made an arrangement with Maximillian of Austria, a widower, and married him by proxy when she was 13 in order to keep control of Brittany.

Charles VIII of France (who was betrothed to Maximillian's daughter) was also interested in Brittany and, since France sat between Austria and Brittany, didn't fancy being wedged between two foreign powers. He launched a military campaign against Brittany and forced the annulment of Anne's marriage to Maximillian. He broke his own engagement and married Anne himself in the Château of Langeais.

This made Brittany a part of France. Anne was fourteen, and apparently, not so happy to be forced to marry Charles. During their marriage they often lived in separate castles, hers being Clos Lucé, near the Château of Amboise, or Blois. Nevertheless, she was almost continuously pregnant during her marriage.

The couple lived in Amboise but, sadly, none of their seven children survived. Either Anne miscarried or the children died at birth or shortly after. Her son next in line for the throne died of measles at three years old. She was devastated.

Anne's husband, Charles VIII, after only eight years of marriage, was running through the castle, hit his head on a door frame, and died before nightfall. He was only 27 years old. According to a previously made agreement, Anne married Charles' heir, Louis XII (who was already married to someone else, but was granted an annulment by the pope to marry Anne.)

Anne of Brittany was the only woman in French history to be queen of France two times. With Louis, Anne had many more pregnancies and two of her children, daughters, survived. She betrothed her daughter, Claude, ironically, to the grandson of Maximillian, to whom she herself had been married by proxy for a brief period. Her wishes were not honored and after her death, and Claude was married to François I, the subsequent king of France.

Anne lived primarily at the Château of Blois. She was highly intelligent and passionate about protecting Brittany's identity and autonomy and spent much of her life in this pursuit. She was also a patron of the arts and a deeply religious woman. She commissioned a Book of Hours, a devotional and prayer book that was popular among the wealthy during that time in history. She was very involved in building projects in the various châteaux where she lived.

Despite her busy and full life, Anne's was one of frequent sadness and tragedy. She was pregnant 14 times in her life but only two of her children survived. By the time she was 36 her body was weakened from so many pregnancies and miscarriages, and she died from kidney stones.

Southeast Loire Valley

As we move south of Amboise and Blois, you'll encounter some remarkable castles. Chenonceau is most notable, but there are others less famous, but still steeped in historical intrigue, treachery, and royal shenanigans. Along the way, you'll pass the lush, green countryside which surround and protect the towns.

Chenonceau This is perhaps the best-known and most-photographed château in the Loire Valley, with its elegant bridge reflected in the River Cher. The castle we see today was built in the early 16th century (1514-1522) in the Renaissance style, though

Château de Chenonceau

previous castles existed there beginning in the 13th century.

There were many different owners, some nobles, some royalty, and most were women. In fact, Chenonceau is known as the château of the ladies. That is, women were the ones who lived there, supervised renovations, and entertained there. The most famous incident at Chenonceau involved Diane de Poitier, mistress of Henry II. He had given Chenonceau to her as a gift. She had the arched bridge built and enlarged the gardens, overseeing the work herself, bringing from other lands many plants that were previously unknown in France, such as melons and artichokes.

After Henry's death, his wife, Catherine de Medici took the château back and sent Diane de Poitiers to occupy Chaumont instead. Catherine continued enlarging both the château and the gardens, adding three stories on top of Diane's bridge. It is the bridge addition that she turned into a beautiful hall for receiving guests. She was known to throw lavish parties. The first-ever fireworks were set off here to commemorate the crowning of her son, Francis II as king of France.

Like so many buildings in the Loire Valley, Chenonceau is beautifully white, since it was built from limestone so abundant in the region. Rumor has it that the stone becomes lighter, not darker, with age. One can see the truth of this all over the Loire Valley.

Getting there: Chenonceau is a few miles drive southeast of Amboise on the D81 (departmental road) in the town of Chenonceaux (with an "X".) There are buses and excursion vans as well that can take you there. (A tourist information bureau in town can help you with anything you need in the area, or questions you may have.) Also, don't forget the list of excursions and tours on page 46, which can help you organize a visit.

Hours: Open weekends from 9 to 4:30. Vaccine pass is required.

Admission to Château and gardens: Adults, 15€. Leaflet guide included. Children ages 7 to 18 and students ages 18 to 27 cost 12€. Children under 7, free. Free for handicapped people and journalists. www.chenonceau.com/ Check the site for online tickets and additional information.

Château by Canoe or rowboat. For an interesting way to see the château from the outside, why not take a 2-hour canoe ride on the River Cher, which surrounds Chenonceau? Choose a morning or sunset tour by canoe. www.canoe-company.fr Longer trips are available to other parts of the Loire and Cher

rivers. Rowboat tours are avai.
through the château. Ask for informau.
the château entrance.

Loches

Loches is a fortified, medieval town, the largest in this area. It sits perched upon a rock and overlooks the river Indre. It is one of the few medieval cities to have most of its 12th century ramparts intact. Loches is about 25 minutes by car due south of Amboise and about 30 minutes southeast of Tours.

Known as a city of art and history, history-lovers will enjoy the town for even more reasons. Here you'll find one of the oldest and largest dungeons in Europe, built around the year 1000. The church of St. Ours (see following) is another fine example of medieval architecture from the 11th century, though it was founded much earlier on a monastery from the 6th century, the first structure built in the city. Its four towers are visible from around the town.

The monastery was built around 500 A.D. The town of Loches grew up around it and flourished in the centuries that followed. In the early days Loches was under the control of the Counts of Anjou and belonged to England for a while, but later in the 13th century it was taken back by Louis Philippe. For most of its history, the château in Loches was property of the kings of France. At various times it was visited by Anne of Brittany and Joan of Arc.

Loches is one of the most picturesque towns in the Loire Valley and is a good base from which to explore this corner of the Valley southeast of Tours.

Seeing and Doing in Loches

Old town Renaissance buildings, including stately mansions, the 16th century city hall, and Antoine Tower, reflect the prosperity of later centuries in the town of Loches. The town is known for (leather) tanning, vineyards, and just strolling around enjoying the historic atmosphere. You can enjoy the open market, which occurs twice a week, and of course, savor the Loire Valley cuisine.

Château/Fortress of Loches This ancient structure has a large, square tower that dominates the town. It is both a royal dwelling and a medieval fortress. The keep (*donjon*, or dungeon but is really more of a keep, originally used for storage) was built in the 11th century by a count of Anjou, Foulques Nerra, in the Romanesque style. It was a residence and a defensive fortress, and in the Middle Ages served as a prison. Later it was a royal castle once King Phillip II got it back in 1204 from English King Henry II and his son Richard the Lionheart. King

Charles VII preferred it to other residences and brought his mistress, Agnès Sorel, to live there.

Getting there: You can't miss it if you are in Loches!

Hours: Open most of the year. From April 1 to September 30, open 9 am to 7 pm. October 1 to March 31, open from 9:30 to 5 pm.

Admission: Adults, 10€50. Children ages 7 to 18 and students, 8€50. Children under 7, free. Paid admission includes *Histopad*, an interactive tablet to guide your visit. (5 € for free entrance.) There may be a 2€50 supplement for special events.

Maison-Musée Lansyer Emmanuel Lansyer was a landscape painter from the 19th century who was born in Loches. A 10-minute movie with subtitles provide background on Lansyer's life and work. You can see the museum in an hour, so it's a nice oasis from tourist visits and castle-hopping. The artist's landscape paintings and engravings are on display and works of other artists as well. Open from 10 am to 6 pm. Address: 1 rue Lansyer, Loches.

Eglise Collégiale St Ours Founded in the 10th century, the building was begun in the 11th century. Additions were done in the 12th century. Once you are inside, you'll see a few interesting architectural features. First, an ornate portal, and second, hollow pyramid-shaped spaces (called *dubes*) going upward to the ceiling. This is exceedingly rare to find in a cathedral. In this church lies the tomb of Agnès Sorel, the first official mistress of a French king. She died in childbirth at the age of 28, but prior to that was a patron of the church and the arts. Outside the church, notice the contrasting look between the end towers and those in the middle.

Confisserie Hallard A half mile from the town center, you'll discover the candy shop that's also a workshop. Come watch candy being made and even enjoy a taste! Traditional flavors, such as nougats, fruit, and pralines, as well as more unusual ones like bergamot, rose, lemon, Coke, and violet. Open daily from April to the end of September except on weekends from 10 am to 12 pm and from 2:30 to 6:30 pm. Address: 62 bis, avenue Aristide Briande, Loches.

Nearby Exploring

Moulins (Mills) des Aigremonts You'll find windmills are just north of Loches in the town of Bléré. This type of mill is found only in the Loire Valley and is still in use. Up to the 19th century, the mill was an integral part of village life. During a guided visit of a flour mill, you can see the mechanics and production of the process of grinding grain to flour as well as a museum to give you the historic overview of flour production.

Address: Rue de Loches, Bléré. www.moulindesaigremonts.com/ . Fall programming is on schedule. Open weekends and holidays from May 1 through September 30th from 10 to 12 and 2 to 4 pm. pm.

Admission: 3€. Free under age 14. More info: Tel. 02.47.30.81.81.

Golf this area is known for several golf courses if you'd like to take a break and practice your swing. One of these is Loches-Verneuil Golf Club.

Zooparc de Beauval is called one of the 10 most beautiful zoos in the world, with 10,000 animals from 600 species. Come see giant pandas (the only pandas in France), elephants, gorillas, koalas, lions, tigers, and many more on acres of beautifully landscaped paths and gardens.

Getting there: located in the town of Saint Aignan-sur-Cher, northeast of Loches (go east to get on route D675 then go north) and 45 minutes south from Blois by route D675.

Hours: Open daily from 9 am to sundown all year, though last tickets are sold at 7:30 pm in summer. Varied hours for exhibits (pandas, tropical hothouse, hippopotamus, and the boutique.) Twelve restaurants are scattered throughout the zoo and are open for lunch.

<u>Admission</u>: One or two-day tickets are available, as are year passes. For one day, Adults 34 €, children ages 3 to 10, 27 €. Children under 3 are free. Save one or two euros if you book online. www.zoobeauval.com/ Get dated or undated tickets. (I love looking at their website!)

Château de Montpoupon This smaller château has been inhabited by the same family since 1857. Though it's near a road, surrounding it are lush green fields. Inside, all the rooms are furnished. Though it was not a château belonging to the king, a room was prepared and reserved for him at all times, should he wish to pay a visit. There is also a 30-room museum dedicated to hunting and equestrian activities, including coaches and carriages.

The castle's oldest part was built in the 12th century. There is a cylindrical keep, typical in medieval times, with small windows and slots at the top to shoot arrows. Some later additions are from the 15th and 16th centuries.

<u>Getting there</u>: Follow the road that connects Loches with Montrichard (Route D764) and you will see it alongside the road. The castle is between Chenonceau and Beauval.

<u>Hours</u>: From April to September, open daily from 10 am to 7 pm. From September 1 to November 6, open from 10 to 6. February 5 to March 6 and weekends

March 12 to 27. November 11 to 27, open weekends from 10 am to 1 pm and 2 pm to 5 pm. Closed December and January.

<u>Admission</u>: Adults, 10€. Children and students under age 26, 7€50. Children ages 5 to 14, 5€. Over age 65, 9€. Family and group rates are available. Admission includes the visit, the museum, and the park.

Staying and Eating in Loches

Staying

<u>Luxury/medium</u>

La Closerie Saint Jacques Bed and Breakfast. 37 rue Balzac, Loches. If you want to really treat yourself, stay in this 17th century manor house bed and breakfast. It's surprisingly affordable. You can book online at: https://closeriesaintjacques.com/

<u>Medium priced</u>

Inter-Hotel Loches George Sand 39 rue Quintefol, Loches; close to the river in central Loches. http://www.hotelrestaurant-georgesand.com/

Les Troglos de Beaulieu 26 rue des Bertrands, Loches. For a unique lodging experience, stay in a troglodyte hotel in a tranquil setting. Breakfast included. troglo-beaulieu.fr/

Eating

Le P'tit Restau As the name suggests, it's a cozy place where you can get locally sourced seasonal and organic meals with a regional flair. A new upstairs adds space for more diners. Lunch menu is a favorite among regulars. 6 Grande Rue, Loches

La Crêpiçoise For your crêpe craving, drop in and dine on crêpes in comfortable surroundings. 3 Rue Picois, Loches. 02 47 59 25 59.

L'Entracte Located in the heart of Old Loches, is open for lunch and dinner from Tuesday to Saturday. They offer local and seasonal products with a menu that changes with the season. Dine inside or on a terrace. Priced between 14€ and 29€90, depending on the number of courses.

Auberge de Monpoupon This homey restaurant with wood beams and stone sits at the base of the Monpoupon castle. The terrace affords views of the castle. Memorable recipes of regional favorites are also reasonably priced, around 25€.
Address: Le Moulin Bailly, Céré-la-ronde.

Southwest Loire Valley

In this area, either of two main cities, Chinon or Saumur, would be ideal as your base city. They are close enough to each other that you can visit both easily, so you can dock in one and visit the other, as well as the many other sites all around. If you'd like some orientation (or get tickets, or make reservations), start your visit at the Tourist Information Bureau, located at 1 rue Rabelais, Chinon. Open 10 to 6 pm. It's closed at lunchtime, 12:30 to 2:30 pm.

Chinon

Like so many of the larger towns in the Loire Valley, Chinon has much historical and royal importance. It lies on the banks of the Vienne River, a tributary of the Loire, which it joins a few miles away. The town itself has prehistoric roots, and the castle was begun in the 11th century, making Chinon a truly medieval town.

In the Middle Ages an English king, Henry II, resided in the royal castle with his wife, Eleanor of Aquitaine. During that time, he had the east wing added. Their son, Richard the Lionheart, was born.

Richard's son lost the castle to the French during a month-long siege in 1205, and it has been French ever since. After that, the French king, Philip Augustus, added new walls and a moat and repaired the towers.

During the Hundred Years War, the Dauphin (son of the king), Charles VII, was based in Chinon. Joan of Arc came to see him in 1429 in hopes of rallying his commitment to reclaiming what he'd lost to the English. Her pep talk worked wonders. He furnished her with men and arms for her march to Orléans, which turned the war in favor of the French. After Charles was crowned king, he made Chinon his capital, which it stayed for a century. During his reign, he abolished the feudal structure, and the castle entered the height of its royal importance.

Later in 1631 the château became the property of the Duke of Richlieu. History shows that this was a bad idea. He tore the castle down and used some of its stones to help build the city of Richlieu, which he created from scratch, proclaiming it a "perfect" city (see page 135.) Fortunately, the destruction of Chinon's castle was never completed. Since 1854 the Chinon Château has undergone much restoration, with the goal of bringing it back to its original state.

Seeing and Doing

Royal Castle of Chinon   The castle sits on a rocky outcrop above the Vienne River. One can easily discern its medieval origins just by looking at it. Parts of it are crumbling, yet it remains almost pristine white, thanks to the building material, the limestone so pervasive in the region. Despite its earlier neglect and near destruction, you can visit the château daily, thanks to massive efforts at renovation over the last century or so.

You can visit and enjoy dramatized tours as well as seasonal museum exhibits. There are self-guided tours with a booklet, guided tours, and iPad tours, giving you an interactive experience. Interactive tablets lead you throughout the château, so even if you choose the self-guided option, you'll deepen your tour experience with a dash of modern technology!

Getting there: The castle is on the right bank of the Vienne River. You can see it from all over the town and can follow the small roads until you get there.

Hours: May 1 to August 31 the castle is open from 9:30 am to 7 pm. March, April, September, and October, open 9:30 am to 6 pm. January, February, November, and December, open 9:30 am to 5 pm.

<u>Admission</u>: Adults, 10€50. Children ages 7 to 18 and college students, 8€50. Under age 7, free.

Old town Chinon This area is on the right bank of the Vienne River at the foot of the château. To learn more about the historic fabric of this fascinating town, take a guided visit through its narrow streets filled with medieval half-timbered houses as well as Renaissance structures. Most of these are on Rue Jean-Jacques Rousseau and Rue Voltaire. Some buildings date from the 14th and 15th centuries, but you'll see architectural styles from the 16th through the 19th centuries as well. Some splendid manor houses of the wealthy from the 15th century sit on Rue du Docteur Gendron and Rue du Grenier à Sel. Some of these mansions' owners added Renaissance features, like turrets and staircases. Have a look on Rue Voltaire and Rue Haute Saint Maurice. Town houses came along later, not until the 19th century. Though the medieval city was once surrounded by protective walls, in the 1820s they were torn down to open and enlarge the town.

Winding streets will lead you up to the castle, where you'll also find scenic detours of gardens and courtyards. Visit the tourist information bureau (1 Rue Rabelais) for more information on visits around the town. Or if you prefer, pick up a map there and just wander around on a quest of discovery.

Eventually your steps will lead you to the Place du General de Gaulle where you'll find an animated square filled with cafés, restaurants, and shops.

You can't miss the beautiful (huge) bronze statue of Joan of Arc in the Square Jeanne d'Arc. It's stunning and full of action, as opposed to some of the humbler, more sedate statues of this great woman of history. It's located in an open area that is also used for the weekly market. Speaking of markets, the third Sunday of each month there is an antiques/flea (brocante) market on the left bank side of the town.

Wine Museum Officially called, Le Musée Animé du Vin et de la Tonnellerie, which means interactive museum of wine and barrel-making. An appropriate theme for this region, since Chinon wines are known throughout the world. Located at 1 rue Voltaire in Chinon. It's also a restaurant with regional choices.

Hours: Open from mid-March to Mid-October from 10 am to 10 pm.

Admission: Adults, 4€50, children ages 7 to 12, 3€50.

Saint Mexme Collegiate Church The oldest parts of this building go back to the year 1000. It was the main religious building of the town up to the Revolution, during which time it was abandoned, and it partially collapsed. A collegiate is a church run by canons, a type of priest. They lived near the church, and you can see their historic homes in this area east of downtown, especially on Rue Diderot, Rue Hoche, and Rue Buffon.

St. Etienne Church (Eglise) This 15th century church replaced an earlier one from the 11th century that was destroyed. The current version has many Gothic features, lovely stained glass behind the altar, and airy vaulted space overhead. Inside is a marble statue of Joan of Arc. It is located at the Parvis St. Etienne, several blocks east of the château.

St. Maurice Church (Eglise) At Place Saint Maurice you'll find its namesake, another church, this one dating from the 12th century

Carroi Museum of Art and History contains archeological collections, including a 12th century piece of Arab silk and medieval statues. Located at 44 rue Haute-St-Maurice. Open June 15 to September 22 from 2:30 pm to 6:30 pm. Admission: Adults, 4 €. Children ages 6 to 18, 2€50. Under 6, free.

Vineyards in and near Chinon

There are many places in the area to taste wine, take a wine tour, and buy wine (even just one bottle.) For a helpful overview of Loire Valley Wines, see pages 176-183.

Cave Plouzeau Located near the château, this wine cellar began as a 10th-century quarry. Today it's a leader in organic farming. Address: 94 rue Haute St. Maurice. Wines produced are AOC Chinon and AOC Touraine. Tastings are free.

Hours: Open from April to September Tuesday through Saturday 11 am to 1 pm and 3 pm to 7 pm. In November, December, February, and March, open Tuesday through Friday from 2 to 6 pm and Saturday 11 am to 1 pm and 2 to 6 pm.

La Cave Mon Plaisir Also near the château and formed from limestone quarries, it provides an exceptional view of an underground (troglodyte) site where it stores over 700 barrels of various kinds of Loire Valley wines. Located on the Quai Pasteur in Chinon. They produce AOC Chinon, AOC Touraine, and AOC Vouvray wines.

Hours: Open daily from July 1 to August 31 from 10:30 am to 7 pm. Low season: March 15 to June 30, and September 1 to November 15, and December 15 to December 31 (except 12/25) open 10:30 am to 12:30 pm, and 2:30 pm to 6 pm. Closed Wednesdays.

Château de la Grille   First, find and admire the lovely 15th century château surrounded by vineyards. Then stroll through the vineyards and finish by tasting Chinon and Touraine wines in the wine-tasting cellar. Guided tours are 6€ for adults and reservations are required. Tastings alone are free. (Guided tours are optional.) Located on the Route de Huismes, Chinon. Www.chateau-de-la-grille.com

Chinon Forest This large forest all around Chinon is a perfect place to bike and hike. Bikes can be rented in town. (Elo Bike Tours; also see biking in the index and special categories section.)

Nearby Exploring

Château du Rivau (6 miles south of Chinon.) This lesser-known but impressively restored 13th-century castle blends both medieval and Renaissance architecture. The castle comes alive during your visit with an audio accompaniment that takes you back in history.

Open in summer 10 am to 7 pm, in spring and fall until 6 pm. Two on-site restaurants are open from April to November (except for dinner) and you can stay there, too! Twelve rooms are available for those who want to sleep in a real castle!

Admission to castle, stables, and gardens: Adults, 12€ for a self-guided tour of the castle and grounds. Children ages 5 to 18, 7€. Students to age 25, 9€50. Special activities for children (3€50 extra) are available. Family passes, discounts for disabled. Audioguide, 3€50.

Musée Rabelais Just about 3 miles from the town of Chinon is the François Rabelais Museum, located in a country cottage. This 15th century building was the birthplace of the famous writer and scholar in 1494. He is best-known for his novel, *Gargantua*. A guided tour is included in the admission price, as well as a game booklet for children and an audioguide. A guided visit is included in admission, but you can also visit on your own. Visits are 11:15, 3:15, 4:30 and 5:30. The museum is located in the town of Seuilly, just southwest of Chinon.

Hours: Open April 1 to June 30 and September 1 to 30, open from 10:30 am to 12:30 pm, and 2 pm to 6 pm. From July 1 to August 31, open 10 am to 7 pm. Fall/winter hours: October 1 to March 31 open 10 to 12:30 and 2pm to 5 pm. Closed Tuesdays. www.musee-rabelais.fr

Admission: Adults, 6€. Children ages 7 to 18, 5€. Children under 7, free.

Château de Villandry Villandry is one of the best-known châteaux in the Loire Valley, thanks to its sumptuous gardens (six in all.) Throughout the gardens you'll find "interpretation stations" to explain what the plants are and what the designs mean. The best time to visit is summer, since in early spring the plantings are not mature and therefore less colorful. You can tour just the gardens, or both the castle and gardens. The château is closer to Tours than to Chinon, so it's a good day trip from either city. The Château of Langeais is right across the river, so grouping these two is a good idea. (Details about Langeais are found in the Northwest section.)

The gardens alone are enough to occupy much of your time, with the herb garden, the water garden, the kitchen (vegetable) garden, the sun garden, the labyrinth, the ornamental gardens, the green houses, and the children's play area. There are even woods surrounding the gardens.

As for the château, it is the last Renaissance Château built in this area. It was not a royal castle, but was the residence of Jean le Breton, finance minister for François I. Inside rooms were renovated in the 18th century and contain furnishings and art to complete your visit. The château restaurant, La Doulce Terrasse, is near the entrance. It uses locally sourced produce and wine.

<u>Getting there</u>: Villandry is located on the left bank of the River Cher, which branches off from the Loire. It's off of the D7 Departmental Road. Villandry is not far from Tours or Saumur.

Château and Gardens at Villandry

<u>Hours</u>: Villandry is open April through June and August through October from 9 am to 6 pm. During July and August, open 9 am to 6:30 pm. Off season months vary. Consult the website. Closed January 4 to February 4. Gardens are open from 9 am to 7 pm during warm weather. Earlier closing otherwise.

<u>Admission</u>: Adults 12€, Children age 8 to 18 and students, 7€. Children under 8 are free. Gardens only: Adults 7€50, children 5€. Audio guides are

available in several languages for 4€. Guided visits in French are available from April to October.

Les Grottes (Caves) Pétrifiantes Just a half mile from Villandry in the town of Savonnières are underground caves (*grottes*), which take you to a surreal-looking world originally discovered in 1547. You'll see underground lakes and limestone stalagmites and stalactites. Address: 61 route des Grottes Pétrifiantes, Savonnières.

Hours: Open daily April to June 30 from 10 am to 7 pm.

Admission: Adults, 7€60, children from 5 to 16, 5€50. Children under 5, free.

Azay-le-Rideau The most remarkable feature of this castle is the fact that it appears to be sitting *in* the Indre River, though actually the water surrounds it and reflects its majesty. The word "rideau" in French means curtain, but the name actually comes from the château's 12th-century owner, Rideau d'Azay. The château you see isn't the original, however. In the early 15th century, it belonged to the Duke of Burgundy. The unfortunate duke offended the future Charles VII (the same king who met with Joan of Arc) and the king sent an army to destroy the castle, the nearby town, and the garrison. It is *very* unwise to offend the king.

A century later in the 16th century it was rebuilt on the same site and includes both Gothic and Renaissance architecture as well as a splash of the Italian influence so popular in the 16th century. The finance minister of François I (the king who built so many castles in the Loire Valley) lived in the Château of Azay and did extensive improvements there. Many of the features you see today were completed in the 19th century.

Much of the château has been restored, especially the furnishings and room décor. In fact, a new renovation has recently been completed.

Getting there: 19 Rue Balzac, Azay-le-Rideau (town). Departmental Road D751, exit 11.

Hours: April 1 to June 30 and September 1 to 30, open 9:30 am to 6 pm. From July 1 to August 31, open from 9:30 am to 7 pm. From October 1 through March 31, open daily at 10 am until 5:15 pm.

Admission: Adults, 11€50; children ages 18 to 26 non E.U. citizens, 8€50. Children under 18, free. Ages 18 to 26 E.U. citizens, free. Audioguide available for 3€ extra.

Musée Balzac This museum dedicated to the writer, Honoré de Balzac (born 1799), is located inside the Château de Saché, where he often stayed as a guest of his friend, Jean Margonne. It is only a few miles from Azay-le-Rideau, due east in the town of Saché. The museum has more than just mementos of the writer's life, but also sculptures, paintings, and manuscripts. The décor is from the 19th century.

<u>Hours</u>: Open daily from April 1 to June 30, and September 1 to 30, open from 10 am to 6 pm. Open from July 1 to August 31 from 10 am to 7 pm. October 1 through March 31 open 10 am to 12:30 and 2 pm to 5 pm and closed Tuesday.

<u>Admission</u>: Adults, 6€. Children ages 7 and older, 5€. Children under 7, free.

Château d'Ussé *(Town is Rigny-Ussé)* If there is a fairytale castle in the Loire Valley, this is it. You'd think so by looking at it, even if you didn't know that it inspired the author of *Sleeping Beauty*, Charles Perrault.

A medieval stronghold dating from 1000 A.D. later (15th century) became the site of the castle. As was the case with many castles of the Loire, construction and renovations continued over the next four centuries. The round towers and slate turrets complete the fairytale castle image.

Château d'Ussé

The castle is furnished with many historical pieces, Flemish tapestries, and weapons. In addition, the story of Sleeping Beauty is portrayed by costumed mannequins throughout the castle. It has been inhabited by the same family for two centuries, and the current owners live on site.

The lovely formal garden was designed by Le Nôtre, who also designed the gardens at Versailles. There, you'll see fountains, citrus trees, palms, flowers, and two cedars of Lebanon. Included in your ticket is a visit to the gardens, the stables, and the chapel. A treasure hunt is available for children.

Getting there: Located in the town of Rigny-Ussé, southwest of Villandry and northeast of Chinon.

Hours: Open April 1 to September 30 from 10 am to 7 pm. Mid-February to March 31 and October 1 to November 1, open 10am to 6 pm.

Admission: Adults, 14 €. Children ages 8 to 16, 5 €. Under 8, free. Admission includes an information sheet in several languages. An audioguide is available for 3 €.

Montreuil-Bellay Château We are beginning to see a common thread among many châteaux, a feudal fortress or stronghold in medieval times becomes the site of a castle centuries later. Many of these ancient fortresses in the region were built by the 11th century Count of Anjou, Foulque (Fulk) Nerra. The Château of Montreuil-Bellay was his work as well, and later given to one of his vassals, Du Bellay. It was a strong, protective enclave during the conflicts between England and France, including a three-year siege. Now privately owned, it has been inhabited by the same family since 1822.

The château is furnished. One clearly sees, outside and in, that it dates to medieval times, though it has been restored. Its current appearance was largely due to building and restoration during the 13th to 15th centuries. During the French Revolution it served as a women's prison, and during World War I, it was a hospital. Today is one of the best-preserved examples of a medieval fortress in the area.

Getting there: The Château Montreuil-Bellay is 10 minutes south of Saumur at Place des Ormeaux in the town of Montreuil-Bellay.

Hours: Open daily from April 1 to June 30 and September, open from 10 am to 12 pm, and 2 pm to 6 pm. During July and August, open from 10 am to 1 pm and 2 to 6:30 pm. October 1 to 22, from 2 pm to 6 pm. During winter months, hours are variable. Check their website. Closed Tuesdays.

Admission: Adults, 11€. Children ages 7 to 18, 6€20. Children under 7, free. Students 15 and older, 10 €. Gardens only, 6€50.

Staying and Eating in Chinon

Staying

La Maison Rouge 1 rue Jeanne d'Arc, Chinon This is a lovely whole apartment (over 1200 square feet) for up to 6 people. It's central location places you close to the château. Enjoy apartment living with many amenities (including parking and WiFi.) It's very popular, so you should reserve far in in advance.

Around 135€ per night. Check their website for current rates and minimum night stay.

Hotel Agnes Sorel   4 Quai Pasteur, Chinon Attractive 2-star hotel is near the river *and* in the old town. Some rooms have a river view. Around 80€ per night depending on season.

Nature et Châteaux   3 Place St Maurice More of an apartment than a hotel, Nature and Châteaux has a fully equipped kitchenette, free parking, and bike rental on site. It's pet-friendly and close to everything. Average cost, 90€ per night. Apartments are also available in Villandry and near Azay-le-Rideau.

Eating

Les Années Trente   78 Rue Haute St. Maurice, Chinon   This picturesque restaurant features artifacts of the 1930s (hence the name, les Années Trente). Quality ingredients expertly prepared, there are 2 menus at prix fixe at 32€ and 45€. A lunch menu is available at 22€ during the week and is served with a glass of wine and coffee. Open at Thursday noon to Monday evening. Hours: 12:15 pm and 7:30 pm.

Au Chapeau Rouge 49 Place du General De Gaulle, Chinon This elegant restaurant has outside dining and classic decor inside and features local and seasonal ingredients in regional specialties. Meals range from 26 to 47€ on average. Open 12 pm and 7:30 pm.

Saumur

At the juncture of the Loire and Thouet Rivers sits the town of Saumur, which is worthwhile, either as your base or as a place to spend the day. Its medieval charm is similar to that of Chinon and Old Tours, and it sits under the watchful eye of the château up on the hillside.

The city has existed since the fourth century as a village called Mur (French for 'wall'.) The town is surrounded by vineyards, which produce Saumur wine in various forms and colors. The Old Town itself will keep you busy as you wander narrow streets, admire half-timbered houses from the 15th and 16th centuries, or wind your steps up toward the château. Saumur is called a "city of art and history" by the minister of French culture.

Office of Tourism: located at 8 bis, Quai Carnot. It is near the river.

Place Saint Pierre It is around this Place that the medieval hum circulates, where you can stop at a café under the trees and half-timbered buildings. Nearby is the Saint Pierre Church and a network of streets from another age.

Eglise Saint Pierre Behind a newly restored façade that dates from the 17th century is actually one of the oldest churches in the area, which demonstrates an evolution in styles (including Gothic Plantagenet and Romanesque) over the centuries. Begun in the 12th century, it has been classed a historical monument since 1862. It's open from 9 am to 7 pm and is free. Located at Place Saint Pierre, which you should not miss either (and where you'll probably have lunch!)

Château de Saumur Before or after you wander the picturesque streets, you'll likely want to climb the hill and visit the château. The earliest beginnings of the château are from the 10th century. It first belonged to counts of Blois and Anjou, then the English Plantagenet family. In 1203 Philip Augustus took ownership and made it a French royal castle. In 1589, Henri IV gave it to Philippe Duplessis-Mornay, his advisor. Duplessis-Mornay was also a champion of Protestantism in France, founding the Protestant Academy in Saumur in 1593. He served as the governor of Saumur under two kings.

Later, the castle fell into disrepair and was used as a barracks, then a prison during Napoleon's reign.

The château was open to the public after its renovation in the early 1900s. Inside the castle, the attraction, aside from the architecture, isn't period furnishings, but the Musée de Saumur, which contains a variety of art types, from ceramics, tapestry, equestrian artifacts, natural science objects, and decorative arts. Each year in late September Saumur hosts a grape harvest festival near the château. Ask about the Fête des Vendanges or harvest festival at the Tourist Information Bureau (page 132) if you're in the area at that time.

Château de Saumur

Hours: Open daily, but closed Monday. February 5 to March 31 and October 1 to December 31 open 10 am to 1 pm and 2 pm to 5:30 pm. April 1 to June 30 and all of September, open 10 am to 6 pm. July 1 to August 31, open 10 am to 7 pm, including Mondays.

Admission: Adults 8€, children between 7 and 16 cost 6€. Children under 7 are free. Family and group tickets are available. A 30-minute guided visit in French or English is available at no extra cost. A game booklet is available for 7 to 12-year-olds. Access to the top of the castle for views of the area, 3€ extra. www.chateau-saumur.fr Website is in French.

Historic Architecture

There are quite a few historic homes of the wealthy you can view from the outside, to get a peek of the lifestyles of the rich in the 15th century, as well as other medieval structures.

Maison des Compagnons (du Devoir) This 15th century house was tumbling down when it was restored and repurposed for a training center for stone masons. It is on Rue Duplessis-Mornay.

<u>Maison du Roi</u> This is a home from the 15th century, inhabited by various kings and queens and later owned by wealthy families of Saumur. 33 Rue Dacier

<u>Hôtel Blancer</u> This home dates from the 15th century. It has a Louis XVI façade.

<u>The Papegault Tower</u> was once part of the old (15th century) town walls.

Two 17th century homes to see: <u>Maison des Ange</u> on Rue Fourrier and <u>Hôtel de Sourdé</u> on Rue du Temple.

Musée des Blindées This may be a first for you in your travels: a museum of military vehicles, tanks, and canons. This will interest military and World War buffs, or anyone who loves history. 1043 rue de Fontevraud. Admission: Adults, 10€. Children ages 7 to 15, 6€. Students, 8€. <u>museedesblindes.fr</u>

La Fête Foraine How about a street festival to add even more fun to your visit? In late March you can enjoy a fair in Saumur, La Fête Foraine. Watch the streets come alive and enjoy the festivity!

Cadre Noir is France's elite national equestrian school, founded in 1771 (current school founded in 1815) for training officers. You can see a limited number of shows from February through early November, or simply take a tour and admire the horses.

The word Noir means black and is due to the black uniforms of the riders (not the horses.) The center resides in the town of St-Hilaire St-Florent, on the western edge of Saumur.

Open Mondays from 2 pm to 5:30 pm, and Tuesday through Friday from 9:30 am to 12:30 and 2 to 5:30 pm.

A classic visit (without a show) is 8€ for adults and 6€ for children under 16. Visits last one hour from 10:30 to 11:30 am or 2:30 to 4 pm. See website for exact dates of visits and shows. Shows are only certain times a year and cost 35€ for adults and 15€ for children. See the Cadre Noir website for more details and current pricing.

www.ifce.fr/cadre-noir/

Cadre Noir Riding School

Vineyards in and near Saumur

Saumur is known for sparkling wines and especially for dry red wines made from Cabernet Franc grapes. Some blends include Cabernet Sauvignon or Pinot d'Aunis, though the Cabernet Franc are the best-known and appreciated. Saumur-Champigny is also a well-liked blend from the region made primarily with Cabernet Franc, as well as Puy-Notre-Dame. The white wine found predominantly in the Saumur region is Chenin Blanc. The limestone caves found all over the region provide an ideal setting for wine-production, especially sparkling wines, due to the porous limestone environment and temperature of the caves. The majority of Saumur wines produced are red.

Saumur Champigny is considered by some to be the best red wine in the Loire Valley. Many beverages could be given this illustrious title, but it's for you to determine!

For tasting, you won't lack places to visit, since vineyards and tasting rooms surround the city. If you visit troglodyte caves or wine cellars, be sure to take a sweater with you so you'll stay comfortable underground. Here are some ideas, and you'll get many more when you visit the tourist office.

Ackerman is Saumur's oldest sparkling wine producer, established in 1811. Find them at 19 Rue Léopold Palustre on the bank of the Thouet River in Saumur. They have a wide variety of wines, including sparkling wines, as well as non-alcoholic and organic ones. You can visit the caves and taste a few wines as well.

Gratien & Meyer Go up the hill to enjoy the specialty of sparkling wine along with a great view of Saumur and the valley. Open all year. In warm months, 9:30 am to 6 pm. Tours can be reserved in advance on the website. Otherwise, just come and taste. Located on the Route de Montsoreau in Saumur.

The Bouvet-Ladubay winery has award-winning wines, especially Brut and sparkling rosé. It is located underneath the 11th century St. Florent Abbey ruins. Tours are available all year. A quiz book will keep kids busy while you're tasting! Address: 1 rue de l'Abbaye, in the town of St Hilaire St Florent (where you also find the Cadre Noir, so you can combine both in one visit if you like.)

As long as you are consuming, be sure to try some Saumur food specialties: A fouée is a type of bread stuffed with goat cheese or pork. Then there are meals with eels, and galipettes, or stuffed mushrooms.

Abbey Frontevraud About 10 miles away from Saumur is a monastery founded in 1101. The impressive complex of buildings is called the Abbey Frontevraud. It is the burial place of the Plantagenet family, including Henry II, Isabella of Angoulême, and Richard the Lionheart. After Henry II's death, his wife, Eleanore of Aquitaine, returned to rule from Frontevraud. It ceased to be a working monastery during the Revolution, and later was a prison.

Abbey Frontevraud

In the center is the main priory, connected to the church, kitchens, and cloisters, all woven through with lush gardens. In addition to being a place of architectural wonder and serenity, there are concerts, conferences, and exhibits throughout the year.

Getting there: The Abbey is off of Route D947, a few miles southeast of Saumur.

Hours: Open all year. From April to October, open 10 am to 7 pm. In July and August, open until 8 pm. January to April and November to December 31, open 9:30 to 6 pm.

<u>Admission</u>: Adults, 12€ for self-guided tour to the abbey and 6€ for the modern art museum. Combine ticket is 15€ for adults. Children under 18 and students under age 25 are free. Discount may be available on presentation of a ticket to a castle in the region (see website under "Partners" for the list.) Tickets are available on site or ordered online. www.fontevraud.fr/en/

There is a restaurant and a hotel on site. Buses are sporadic, so you may wish to rent a car for your visit.

Château de Brissac is currently a 16th century castle in the Renaissance and baroque styles, though in its previous life it was a medieval fortress until 1434. At that time, it was purchased by Pierre de Brézé, who was a minister under Charles VII and Louis XI. Only two cylindrical towers in the Gothic style remain from the original structure.

It is the tallest château in France, with seven stories and 204 rooms. It has been in the same family since 1502, when Pierre de Brézeé sold the castle to René de Cossé. It is gorgeous outside as well as inside, with period furnishings, paintings, and tapestries. Signs of the Italian Renaissance are visible here, as in other châteaux in the region. Surrounding the grounds is a lovely canal, and beneath it is a wine cellar where you can taste Rosé d'Anjou.

<u>Getting there</u>: Rue Louis Moron in the town of Brissac-Quincé.

<u>Hours</u>: Open from Late March to Late June and all of September, 10 am to 1pm and 2 pm to 6 pm. During July and August, open 10 am to 6 pm. During July and August, open 10 am to 5 pm. Reduced hours in low season. Closed Tuesdays.

<u>Admission</u>: Tickets include a guided castle visit (1 hour 15 minutes), the park, wine tasting, and underground tunnel. Adults, 11 €. Children ages 8 to 16, 4 €. Under 8, free. Tickets for park, kitchen, and tunnel only are available for 5€50.

Nearby Exploring

Mushroom Caves By this time you may be well aware of how important mushroom cultivation is in the Loire Valley. After the limestone was mined to build the châteaux, underground caverns were left behind . . . perfect for growing mushrooms. If you'd like to see some mushroom caves, here are a couple of addresses near Saumur.

Cave Vivante du Champignon Guided visit (French or English) in a mushroom cave throughout days of operation and mushrooms for sale all year. Find them in the town of Sanziers, several miles southwest of Saumur. 1 rue du Château, in the town of Le Puy-Notre-Dame. Adults, 7 €. Children ages 6 to 16, 4€.

Le Saut aux Loups This mushroom farm is due east of Saumur in the town of Montsoreau. A one-hour guided visit takes you through 17 rooms. A restaurant on site overlooks the river and specializes (surprise!) in stuffed mushrooms. Open February to November from 10 am to 6 pm (until 7 in July and August.) Adults 7€50, Children 4 to 18, 6€. Restaurant is open for lunch from 12 pm to 2:30 pm. Warning: Wear a sweater to the caves.

River Cruise (Une Croisière) From April to October you can take a boat tour or dinner cruise with the company, Les Docks de la Loire, at 5 rue Bonnemère. Two trips to other towns are also available, by a "navette", or shuttle. Drop by their office for times (the best idea, since the office is close to the embarking point) for cruise schedules, which change depending on the day and month.

You can also show up at the riverbank just past the City Hall. For a 50-minute cruise, rates are 16€ for adults and 8€ for children under 15. Family rate, 40€ for 2 adults and 2 children. Sunset cruise, 25€ and kids, 12€. Dinner cruises are 58€ for adults and 25€ for children under 15. Family passes are available. www.croisieressaumurloire.fr/

Troglomania This is *my* term for the number of underground caves available along the banks of the Loire in Saumur. Some of these are underground towns or restaurants, some are for winemaking and tasting, and still others for cultivating mushrooms. Some have sculptures made of the soft limestone you see all throughout the Loire Valley. Most of these establishments welcome visitors and provide tours. You can get a full listing and info on other ideas in the region at the ***Office of Tourism***. Address: 8 bis Quai Carnot, near the riverfront.

Staying and Eating in Saumur

Staying

Hotel Saint Pierre (Saumur) a 17th century private house is now a four-star hotel with 14 beautiful rooms and one suite. A gourmet breakfast is served (extra cost) in an elegant dining room. Check website for rates and specials.
saintpierresaumur.com

Château Bouvet-Ladubey This small 19th century castle has 5 gorgeous guest rooms as well as the more economical "gite" apartment on the ground floor, with kitchen included. The castle was built by the producers of wine by the same name. You can also enjoy the surrounding park, a pool, and a

conservatory. www.chateaubouvetladubay.com/en/
This B & B is offered through several tourist sites, so
search for the best deal.

Qualys-Hôtel Le Londres-Hôtel & Appartements 48,
rue d'Orleans Begun in 1837, Le Londres Hotel has
undergone an impressive series of renovations, the
most recent of which was completed only in 2016.
This 3-star hotel has rooms of all types (all sizes,
deluxe rooms, family suites, apartments with
kitchenette), as well as a restaurant, tearoom, and
spa. The rate seems very reasonable, with all these
amenities included. Each room has a unique décor.
Close to the castle, center of town, and pedestrian
streets. www.lelondre.com

Kyriad Saumur Centre This is a respectable French
chain, so the quality should be consistent. Clean and
pretty, room rate includes parking and wifi. Three
stars. Breakfast and dinner available on site. 23 rue
Daille. www.kyriad.com/en/hotels/kyriad-saumur-
centre

Eating

Le Gambetta 12 Rue Gambetta This restaurant has
an original flair and a Michelin star, assuring you a
delicious meal. Open for lunch at 12 and for dinner
at 7:15 pm. Closed Sunday and Monday. They have
cooking classes too!

L'Escargot 30 Rue du Maréchal LeClerc This Michelin-awarded restaurant with a fixed price menu at 34€. Terrace dining available; fresh local ingredients. Open at 12 for lunch and 7:30 pm for dinner.

L'Alchemiste 6 rue de Lorraine Refined, traditional cuisine in a modern setting. Pricing between 24€ and 27€. Closed Sunday and Monday.

"Ideal" City of Richlieu

Armand Jean du Plessis (1585-1642) became the powerful Cardinal-Duc de Richlieu, second in power only to the king of France. He served as advisor for King Louis XIII.

Though Cardinal Richlieu was born in Paris, his ancestors lived in a village a few miles south of Chinon, where young Richlieu often went as a child. He purchased the village and determined to make it an "ideal city." In this pursuit he laid out the city on a grid, a new method at the time, and one that would be modeled by other cities in subsequent generations. He also hired Jacques Lemercier, the king's architect and the man who designed the Sorbonne and Le Grand Palais in Paris, to put his magic touch on the town of Richlieu, as well as design and build a sumptuous palace.

It was a walled city (made partially with stones from the Château of Chinon, which Richlieu bought and proceeded to dismantle.) Construction began in 1631, with an emphasis on symmetry. The town is small, about two square miles, and is surrounded by ornamental moats.

The Cardinal attracted new residents to the town by exempting them from taxation, though they had to build their homes according to strict guidelines that would match the perfection of the city. It was a frequent destination for famous figures such as Voltaire and Jean de la Fontaine, both French writers.

Richlieu's enormous château was dismantled in the 19th century and the stones sold. One could say what goes around comes around. Today only walled gardens remain, along with an outbuilding. The building is now a small museum, and the grounds are a park open to the public. On the current château property there are 26 marked hiking trails. You can get details about these at the Saumur Tourist Bureau.

Northwest Loire Valley

As you look at the Loire Valley map, you'll see several more châteaux you can visit in the Northwest section, though these are not as well-known or as numerous. Nevertheless, several are worth a visit, and there are cities and other attractions that will draw you north to this area called Anjou.

Anjou is a historical region in France that is now called Maine-et-Loire, after the rivers that are so central here. **Angers** was the capital of the Anjou region prior to the Revolution. During the medieval period, the city enjoyed the prestige brought by the Plantagenet dynasty and the Dukes of Anjou, both of whom made it their headquarters for governing. Later, the French monarchy moved around the Loire Valley, in Chinon, Amboise, Blois, then gradually settled in Paris.

Angers

Contemporary Angers teems with economic and academic life, sprawling along the Maine River, which flows into the Loire to the south. The proximity of everything in the Loire Valley makes Angers just a short drive away from wherever you are.

When you visit Angers, you'll probably want to pack up and move there, drawn by its history, its lively student and economic rhythm, its art and architecture, and a lot more. Angers isn't just a place to see, it's a place to live. It's a town that stretches across centuries, yet has safeguarded aspects of each one, visible around you as you stroll, explore, and admire.

City of Angers

Today, Angers is home to nearly 150,000 residents, including 40,000 university students. There are several illustrious universities and an important number of companies specializing in biotech and medical research. If you want to study French in a French university, this is your place, at the

International Center for the Study of the French Language.

Most people who visit Angers are attracted to its narrow roads of history in the shadow of 13th, 14th, and 15th-century homes and the medieval castle up on the hillside. It's a fabulous feast of architecture, medieval up to the present. Some remnants of the 13th-century city walls are still visible. Many museums in Angers are housed in historic buildings that are themselves a feast for the eyes.

It is in Angers that you can see the oldest medieval tapestry in the world, and one of the longest. The tapestry entitled *Tenture de l'Apocalypse*, based on the Biblical book of Revelation, is 460 feet long and makes its home inside the Angers castle. In contrast, another tapestry from the 19th century is called *Chant du Monde* and can be seen in the Jean Lurçat Museum. (See more details about both further in the chapter.)

It's easy to get around in Angers, with 24 city buses and a tram. You'll probably wish to see the Old Town, where you can wander for hours admiring Renaissance period buildings from the 15th through the 17th centuries (see a short list below), especially in the sector called La Doutre, and the bustle of the Place de la Laiterie. Here, cafés, restaurants, and shops keep the area humming. The word *laiterie* comes from the word *lait*, or milk. In the old days dairy farmers came to this square to sell their products, and the name stuck.

In nearby Place du Tertre Saint Laurent there are more recent upscale homes from the 19th century. To reach Old Angers from the château, find Rue Beaurepaire and cross the river to the north bank.

If you're looking for a peaceful green area, Le Berges de Maine is a 700-acre park alongside the river.

Medieval and Renaissance Architecture

In Angers there is an impressive number of well-preserved homes from the 15th to 17th centuries that once belonged to the city's wealthy residents (the bourgeoisie.) Older establishments, convents, and monasteries dating from the 12th century and earlier, are likewise scattered around this modern city. Architecture and history buffs, this is your place!

- 15th and 16th-century homes on Rue Beaurepaire, including the Pharmacie de Simon Poisson, from 1582. The carvings on the front demonstrate four virtues.

- Eglise de la Trinité: a cathedral from the 12th century.

- Abbaye de R007Ceray: Located at the Passage de la Censerie, this was the only women-only abbey in Angers. It dates from the 11th century with additions in the 16th century.

- Logis de Maître Sabart, a lovely home from 1482.

- Rue Gruget and Rue Pinte have several note-worthy buildings.

- Rue des Tonneliers is worth a look.

- Lower end of Rue Lionnaise shows a typical street of old Angers, with homes from the 16th century.

- On Rue de la Harpe there is the Couvent des Augustins, a convent, and the Hôtel de Montiron from 1638, which provides lodging for nuns.

- On Rue Vauvert you'll see impressive towers made of stones with roofs of slate, dating from the 15th century

- Hôtel de Pui Gaillard monastery, from 1646.

- At the Place du Tertre, houses from the 15 to 17th centuries, including 12 Place du Tertre, a lovely one from the 16th century.

- On Rue de la Censerie, there are medieval passages and 15th century archways. You'll feel like you've stepped back in history.

- Homes for the rich were often called hôtels. Hôtel du Petit Riveau (15th century), Hotel du Guesclin (date is 1554, but the façade dates from the 17th), Hôtel Gohier de la Jarrilaie, 16th century, Hôtel de Tinteniac, 15th century, on 9-11 Rue Malsou.

As you can see, there is a lot to look at if you are interested in medieval and Renaissance homes and how people lived back in those days.

One modern example that is remarkable is called the Maison Bleue d'Angers. In 1925, Art Déco was all the rage. The economy was down and labor was inexpensive, so many wealthy home-owners took the opportunity to embellish their homes. The Maison Bleue is an example of this, with mosaic and gold on the outside of this 7-story building. Now it has privately-owned apartments, so you can't see inside, but this video clip will show you around one of them, where you'll see the art deco theme from the doors all the way down to the floors. www.youtube.com/watch?v=IReY1Enu6TY

Château d'Angers The Château d'Angers is distinctive in its appearance in a couple of ways. If you've seen pristine fairy-tale castles such as Ussé, by comparison, the Château d'Angers sits in bulky intimidation on the hillside, looking fully medieval. You'll have no trouble believing it was begun in the 9th century and has been an impregnable stronghold throughout history. The outer walls are nearly 10 feet thick.

Château d'Angers

The other aspect is the striped towers, either white (again, limestone) with horizontal "stripes" of darker stone, called schist, or the opposite pattern. The 17 towers that surround the structure are fat with flat-tops, though at one time in the past they were taller. There are two drawbridges for access. You'll also get a glimpse of the more attractive elements, the gardens (formerly the moats), the slate-roof "châtelet" entrance, and the Renaissance chapel.

During the 12th century the English Plantagenet family ruled here, but later in 1204 the castle was taken over by French king Phillip II, who enlarged it. The subsequent Henry III wanted to demolish the castle, using some of the stones from the towers to build roads in Angers, but he didn't succeed, and later rulers halted that process, so the castle remains.

In 1373 Louis I, the Duke of Anjou, commissioned the Apocalypse Tapestry, the longest medieval tapestry in the world, and this is currently on display inside the castle. In the early 15th century, a chapel was added. It was completed in 1382. In addition to seeing the remarkable tapestry, which fills an entire room, you can walk along the ramparts all around the castle.

Getting there: The château is a 10-minute walk from the train station. It is located at 2 Promenade du Bout du Monde, on the south bank of the Maine River. It's a one-hour train ride from Tours, and one and a half hours from Saumur.

Hours: Open from May 2 to September 4 from 10 am to 6:30 pm. From September 5 to April 30 the castle is open from 10 am to 5:30 pm.

: Adults, 9€50. Children under 18, free. To age 26, 7€. E.U residents ages 18 to 26 are free. Audio guide, 3€.

Musée Jean Lurçat This art museum resides in what was once a 12th century hospital. Though the architecture itself is something to see, with lovely, vaulted ceilings, the main attraction is Lurcat's *Chant du Monde*, ten modern tapestries inspired by the Apocalypse tapestries. Located at 4 Boulevard Arago. Open daily 10 am to 6 pm. Closed Mondays. Admission: Adults, 6 €.

Musée de Beaux Arts (Fine arts Museum) Still on the theme of art, this fine art museum is housed in the 15th century Logis Barrault building, which once belonged to banker Olivier Barrault, king's treasurer, and mayor of Angers. Inside you'll see the beautiful, vaulted hall, Gothic fireplace, and other memorable features. The museum is considered one of the finest regional museums in France. Along with art and archeological finds from Angers' history, there is a good collection of European masters, Flemish, French, German, and Italian.

Located at 14, rue du Musée, in the historic city center. Open daily 10 am to 6 pm. Closed Monday.

Admission: Adults, 6€. Children under 26, free.

Galerie David d'Angers A native of Angers, 18th century sculptor Pierre-Jean David, better known as David d'Angers, was a world-renowned artist who rivals Michelangelo. His truly amazing works are housed in the 13th-century Toussaint Abbey Church,

Bust of Goethe

though subsequent centuries contributed their architectural styles as well. The museum is located at 33 bis Rue Toussaint and is worth a look, both for the building and the impressive sculptures inside. The medieval space has been covered by a glass roof, which blends modern and ancient, and shines natural light on the jaw-dropping works, many of

146

which were commissioned by heads of other countries. His work can be found all over the world. Open 10 am to 6 pm.

<u>Address</u>: 33 bis rue Toussaint, Angers

<u>Hours</u>: Open Tuesday through Sunday, 10 am to 6 pm.

<u>Admission</u>: Adults, 4€. Children under age 26, free.

Cathédral d'Angers As is the case with many cathedrals and châteaux in the region, this building was begun in the Middle Ages but underwent changes that reflect various styles of architecture over the centuries. 4 rue St. Christophe.

Maison d'Adam This Renaissance building from the late 15th century is popular with visitors. The tall, half-timbered building is the oldest home in Angers. It sits behind the Cathédrale Saint-Maurice and towers over the Place Saint Croix. One of the notable features of the house is a variety of wood sculptures carved into the columns of the house's façade. On one corner of the ground floor is a Tree of Life sculpture, where the building gets its name. A collection of other images ranges from religious to off-color, and many more which depict daily life in medieval times. The sculptures are in remarkably good condition, considering their age.

Maison d'Adam (House of Adam)

Terra Botanica Extraordinary Gardens How about a theme park based on plants? This park opened in 2010 and features 300,000 plants. There is plenty to interest children and teens, as well as the whole family, including a strange and unusual plant exhibit, the butterfly greenhouse, and a T-Rex dinosaur reproduction. You can even go up in a tethered hot-air balloon. A restaurant, La Table du Roi René, is available for hunger cravings.

Getting there: located on the Route d'Epinard in Angers.

Hours: Open all-year round. Open daily in July and August from 10 am to 7 pm. For other months, see the website. www.terrabotanica.fr/en/

Admission: Adults full price, 18€, children ages 4 to 17, 14€50. Family and 2-day passes are available. Ticketing online (at a discount) or on site.

Musée-Château de Villevêque This museum is an annex to the Beaux Arts museum and contains the impressive private collection of the house's late owner, Daniel Duclaux. The displayed works include paintings, furniture, tapestry, sculpture, engravings, manuscripts, and earthenware from a variety of countries and epochs. The 19th century home where the museum resides was built on the ruins of a 12th century defensive castle, of which only the moat remains. The adjoining cloister is open to the public.

Hours: April 9 to July 3 and September 1 to 18, open weekends from 2 to 6 pm. From July 4 to August 31, open Tuesday to Sunday from 2 to 6 pm.

Getting there: Located at 44 rue du General De Gaulle

Admission: 4€ adults, 2€ children.

Cointreau, Anyone? About two miles from the center of Angers in the town of Saint-Barthelemy-d'Anjou is the world's only distillery for the delicious orange-flavored triple sec liqueur, Cointreau. The establishment is called *Carré Cointreau*. Since 1875 Cointreau has been served as an apéritif and digestif and contains 40% alcohol. You can learn how it is made during a 90-minute tour with the help of an iPad. After the tour you can taste different varieties and even purchase some at a discount.

Getting there: located at Boulevard Les Bretonnières, ZI (Zone Industrielle) St. Barthélemy d'Anjou.

Hours: The boutique is open Tuesday through Saturday, from 10 am to 6 pm. Paid tours are available upon reservation online.

Jardin des Plantes This English-style botanical garden and municipal park sits on about 10 acres (4 hectares) and provides a peaceful getaway in nature. The park includes paths, waterfalls, a lake, and many exotic plants and flowers. There are even goats, deer, and an aviary for parrots. Perfect for a picnic! Located at Place Pierre Mendès France, 39 Rue Boreau, Angers.

Nearby Exploring

Château du Plessis-Bourré   Surrounded by water and waterways, this traditional-looking château, with its round towers and pointy slate roofs, can be seen from the road. Unlike most others, it didn't experience massive renovations, destructions, and rebuilding. Though it was built in the late Middle Ages, Renaissance touches were added in later years. Many films have been made here.

The château was built in 1468 and purchased by finance minister to Louis XI, Jean Bourré. Painted panels, Flemish tapestries, and lavish interiors await you. Weddings are often held here, and each December there is a Christmas Market.

The château is near Angers in the town of Ecuillé.

Hours: During February, March, and October, and November, the castle is open from 2 pm to 6 pm. During April, May, and June, it's open from 10 to 6 on Wednesday through Sunday (2 to 6 on Tuesday.) From July 1 to August 29, open 10 am to 6 pm. Visit is self-guided, though guided tours are available in French. Tour translation sheets are available in 5 languages. Closed Mondays.

Admission: For self-guided tours, Adults 10€, children ages 7 to 18, 7€. For guided tours, Adults 12 €, children ages 7 to 15, 9 €. Under age 7, free.

Château de Langeais As with so many other castles in the Loire Valley, the Château de Langeais to the west of Tours holds a turbulent history, on both a personal and architectural level. Fulk Nerra (see page 158), count of Anjou in the 10th century, built a bastion on the hill, which was the first stage of what is currently a Renaissance castle. Two walls of the original structure remain and are in the park adjoining the current castle.

The castle belonged to the House of Anjou and then the Plantagenet Dynasty until 1206 when, following a military victory, it became part of French royal holdings. In subsequent centuries the castle belonged to several owners, English, French, royalty, and wealthy citizens. The castle was torn down by Charles VII in 1428 and rebuilt by Louis XI later in the 15th century, with many features you see today.

In 1491 an important event happened in the castle, the marriage of Charles VIII to Anne of Brittany. With the marriage, the duchy of Brittany became part of France.

Between the end of the 15th century and the early 19th century, the château was not properly maintained. A Parisian lawyer bought it and carried out renovations and repairs, adding to the structure. This work was continued by subsequent owners until it was donated to the French Institute as part of France's historical heritage.

Today you can visit the richly furnished rooms, see a re-enactment of the wedding of Anne and Charles in wax figures and a light and sound show, and admire the 15th and 16th century tapestries and other period works of art.

In the park, there are reproductions of scaffolding and lifting machines which show medieval castle construction methods.

Getting there: Address is Place Pierre de Brosse, Langeais. The castle is on the north bank of the river, west of Tours. Langeais is also close the châteaux of Villandry and Rigny-Ussé, if you want to make a loop of nearby sites.

Hours: The castle is open all year. During February and March, open at 9:30 am to 5:30 pm, April through June, September until November 11, open from 9:30 to 6:30 pm. July and August open 9 am to 4 pm. November 12 to January 31, open from 10 am to 5 pm. Christmas day open from 2 pm to 5 pm.

Admission: For high/low season, Adults, 11€/10€ Children ages 10 to 17, 5€20/5€. Ages 18 to 25, 9€/8€. Children under 10, free. Admission includes an information card available in several languages. Guided tours are available in French and last one hour. High season is April 1 to November 11.

Le Château du Lude Le Lude is a truly beautiful château situated a few miles northwest of Langeais and of Tours on the north side of the Loire. Like the castle of Langeais, it was begun in the 10th century. Through renovations in the 13th century, the castle acquired a keep, six towers, and a moat. Of the medieval structures, only an underground vaulted room remains today. In the 15th century more renovations were done to transform a feudal fortress to a more comfortable château.

Subsequent owners added new wings and ornamentation in the Renaissance style. Décor, gardens, and architecture (inside and outside) are worth a visit, even if the château is a bit out of the way. Its garden, with terraced and suspended plantings, as well as a Chinese rose garden, greenhouses, and fruit trees, received the "Remarkable Garden" award from the French Ministry of Culture. In early June the annual Garden Festival takes place.

Getting there: 4, Rue Jehans de Daillon, Le Lude.

Hours: Open daily from April through September weekdays from 11 am to 12:30 and 2:30 pm to 6 pm. From October, from 2:30 pm to 5:30 pm. Closed Wednesday in September and October.

Admission: Castle and garden, Adults, 11€. Children ages 7 to 15, 6€. Students, 8€50. Under 7, free.Group rates are available. Garden only, Adults 6€, Children, 4€.

Staying and Eating in Angers

Staying

Hotel le Progrès. This three-star hotel is close to the train station in Angers. It has a very central location, free bicycles, and an on-site bar. A buffet breakfast is available at extra charge. Small but clean and has attractive rooms. 26 rue Denis Papin, Angers. From 65€ per night.

Hotel de France. A Four-star hotel in Angers. 8 Place de la Gare. Close to the train station and central Angers, this hotel has pretty rooms with modern décor and a nice breakfast bar. From 135€ to 192€. A family suite is available.

La Conciergerie Apartement Privé & Spa. 25 rue du Canal, Angers. Fully equipped apartments in a variety of sizes and modern décor. Spa available on site. From 92€ per night. Very central location.

Le Mouton. If you want to get away from the city but not be *too* far away, surrounded by lush greenery as you stay in a historic bed and breakfast, Le Mouton may be just right for you. Swimming pool, 5 beautifully appointed rooms and suites, breakfast or dinner outside on the terrace. Choose between rooms or suites. Location: Porte de Vallée in the town of Blaison Gohier, a few miles south of Angers on the south side of the Loire, near the Château de Brissac. High season rates (2-day minimum for high season): 135€ to 225€, depending on the room. High season is from May 1 to October 1. Low season rates range from 110€ to 165€. Low season is from October 2 to April 30. Bicycling and golf packages are available. A restaurant is on site, open 5 days per week. www.le-mouton.fr

Eating

Le Pois Gourmand, Angers 42 Ave. Besnardière, Angers. Traditional French cuisine from 22 to 30€. Michelin-approved.

Autour d'un Cep, 9 rue Baudrière, Angers. From 42€ to 60€. Traditional French cuisine. Open Monday through Friday.

Aux Jeunes Pousses, 4, rue d'Anjou, Angers. One lengthy fixed menu at 48€ with modern regional cuisine. Prepare to spend about 3 hours!

Ronin, 19 rue Toussaint, Angers. Vegan cuisine at its finest. Enjoy an 8-course set menu with Asian influences. 75€.

Fulk III, also known as Fulk the Black, (the old French spelling was Foulque Nerra), was known as a great builder in the pre-medieval times. His building projects spanned the entire Loire Valley and served as the foundation upon which many of the later Loire Valley castles were built. Fulk was an early Count of Anjou, the region that now encircles the city of Angers. He was a powerful ruler during the Angevin Dynasty of the 10th century and reigned for 53 years as a vassal to the king.

Fulk was also a warrior. He was gifted in military strategy and very successful, though also known to be ruthless and destructive. This destruction was followed by his need to do penance, and he made several trips to the Holy Lands for pilgrimage. Back then, traveling to the Holy Land from France took about six months and was very dangerous. He did this four times. Apparently, he needed a lot of penance. Fulk also founded or repaired several monasteries (though he destroyed a few of them too.)

During his lifetime, Fulk built an estimated 100 medieval fortresses of wood, which were later fortified with stone. The first of these was Langeais, and some remains of his early fortress are still visible on the property of the current Château of Langeais, as well as at Loches. He was known as Foulque le Bâtisseur, or Fulk the Builder.

Fulk was married twice. (He had his first wife executed for adultery.) One of his children, Geoffrey Martel, succeeded him after his death. Several generations later, one of Martel's descendants married Matilda, heir to the English throne. This marriage would eventually produce some members of the House of Plantagenet, the line of English kings, which later contributed to the Hundred Years War between England and France.

More Fun in the Valley

In this section you'll find a treasure trove of resources, beginning with a chart of the Loire Valley castles, which will help you to choose from the abundant array. The chart will list each by area and provide a few distinguishing details.

Here you'll also find the food and wine guide, as well as some resources for nature enthusiasts.

And if you've ever wanted to stay in a château yourself, this section will help you pick your favorite.

Loire Valley Châteaux at a Glance

Château	Location/ Section	Page #	Main Characteristics
Amboise	Northeast	50	François I
Angers	Northwest	142	Medieval
Azay-le-Rideau	Southwest	112	Surrounded by water
Blois	Northeast	70	4 architectural styles, royal
Brissac	Southwest	129	Tallest
Chambord	Northeast	79	Biggest, royal
Chaumont	Northeast	54	Catherine de Medici
Chenonceau	Southeast	90	Best-known/ bridge on water
Cheverny	Northeast	82	Dogs, tulip gardens
Chinon	Southeast	103	Medieval
Clos Lucé	Northeast	52	Da Vinci
Langeais	Northwest	151	Royal, medieval
Le Lude	Northwest	152	Renaissance; gardens
Loches	Southeast	94	Royal, medieval
Montpoupon	Southeast	98	Hunting museum
Montreuil-Bellay	Southwest	116	Medieval, furnished
Saumur	Southwest	120	Royal, medieval
Ussé	Southwest	114	Sleeping Beauty
Villandry	Southwest	109	Many gardens

Château Hotels

Do you want to stay in a castle-hotel in the Loire Valley? Here are some choices both to the east and to the west of Tours.

East of Tours

1. Amboise. *Le Choiseul Hôtel-Restaurant* 36 Quai Charles Guinot, Amboise. Near the center of Amboise, this four-star hotel has 30 rooms and an award-winning restaurant on site. Check their website for specials.

2. Near Tours, Amboise. *Art Hotel* The name seems modern, but don't worry. The hotel, with 28 rooms, is inside the Château de la Taisserie, in the town of Rochecorbon. Near Tours. www.art-hotel-tours.com

3. Amboise. *Le Château des Arpentis* (10 rooms) A peaceful getaway, yet not far from Amboise. This chateau has endured for centuries but provides modern and beautiful comfort. Route D31 in the village of Saint Règle.

4. Tours, Amboise. *Château de la Bourdaisière* 25 rue de la Bourdaisiere, Montlouis-sur-Loire. From the grounds to the rooms, pure elegance. www.labourdaisiere.com

5. Northwest of Amboise, under two miles away. *Château de Perreux* 36 rue de Pocé, Nazelle-Négron. 11 rooms, plus activities, a lovely park, and a restaurant. www.chateaudeperreux.fr

6. Amboise. *Château de Pray,* rue du Cèdre, Chargé (east of Amboise). Has 19 gorgeous rooms, a restaurant. www.chateaudepray.fr

7. Near Amboise, *Chateau de Vallagon* 62 Route de Vallagon, Bourré. 12 rooms in this 3-star hotel, with a pool, playground, and surrounding park. http://chateaudevallagon.fr/en/

See also Château du Breuil, page 85

West of Tours

Near Chinon or Saumur

1. *Château de Marçay*, near Chinon in the town of Marçay, offers 28 elegant rooms, 6 of which are in outbuildings of the château and ideal for families. A restaurant is on site, and the surrounding grounds offer a pool, tennis, pétanque, and wine tasting from the Château vineyard. Massage is also available. To book, call 33 (0)2 47 93 03 47 or email marcay@chateaudemarcay.com

2.   *Château de Verrière* (Hotel and spa, 5 stars) Saumur. Built in 1896 and is close to the Cadre Noir. Located at 53 rue d'Alsace, Saumur. 6 rooms decorated in Belle Epoche style, and a spa to fully relax you. Breakfast is available but not included.

3.   *Château de Noirieux* This lovely 15th century château is located about 10 miles/18 km north of Angers in the town of Briollay, France. It is surrounded by acres of peaceful gardens and forests. A restaurant, pool, and tennis court are on site. To reserve, call 1-800-735-2478 or reserve on their website. (Part of Relais & Châteaux network.)

See also Château Bouvet-Ladubey, Saumur page 132.

For other options, visit Relais & Châteaux, an association of over 500 hotels and restaurants all over France and the world distinguished by elegance and luxury.
www.relaischateaux.com

The Nature Scene

Biking, Walking, Camping, Boating

Biking in the Loire

France is a country that has built an entire tourist industry around biking (called vélo tourisme; a vélo is a bike), creating routes, signage, and all the comforts for bikers. The Loire Valley is a popular area for biking, thanks to peaceful, pastoral landscapes and flat roads, which make easier riding for the whole family (and a variety of fitness levels.) If you are a serious bike-rider, you may be interested in a biking holiday. If you're not, you might still enjoy adding one or more short excursions to a nearby château or vineyard.

There are cycling tour companies (Backroads, Loire Valley Breaks, and others) that will arrange everything for you: itineraries, rentals, housing, and meals. If you'd rather arrange your own biking activities, don't worry, the Loire Valley is well-equipped. They have numerous routes that are clearly indicated, maps, and biking "partners", that is, bike shops, lodging, and other amenities, all over the area. Look for the "acceuil vélo" sign for certified establishments.

There are also numbered itineraries available, which you can find in Tourist information bureaus. For itineraries look for a small green sign with a stick figure on a bike, with the words, "Loire à Vélo", or else by region, for example "L'Anjou à Vélo". One bike route that is known as EuroVélo 6 crosses France through the middle, starting at the Atlantic coast and ending up in Alsace.

Check this link for general information and an itinerary along the whole valley for nearly 500 miles (800 km.) You can choose the segment you want. There's helpful information on where to stay, rent bikes, and routes. The link is the official source for biking information in general around France and will also be helpful for other activities all over the Loire Valley. en.francevelotourisme.com/. Look for

166

the heading Pays de la Loire from the destination drop-down menu.

If you are in the westernmost part of the Loire Valley in a region known as Vendée there is even a phone app available for bicyclists. The previous website gives information on this and other practical helps, such as where to rent bikes. I recommend that you reserve bikes in advance, since it is so popular.

The entire route is signposted for bikes, and two-thirds of it parallels the river. There are 300 stopping places for bikes along this itinerary. Each year about 800,000 cyclists take this route, though about two-thirds of these are French. (Biking has always been a favorite French activity!)

A regional train parallels the river from Orléans to Le Croisic. You can get on and off, as well as take your bike aboard. The Interloire Train is especially accommodating to biking. Many companies exist to transport your luggage as well. The previous sites will give you some tips on finding them.

If you aren't accustomed to biking or aren't very physically active back home, consider a shorter half-day rental before investing in more. Same goes for if you have children with you or others in your party who aren't as fit, or not up for a long ride. Of course, you can always stop as often as you like if you are traveling on your own, which may be one big advantage. Here is a website that provides helpful tips for biking, including where to stay, campgrounds, renting bikes, and much more. www.freewheelingfrance.com/

A baggage transfer service is available through many bike rental companies and "acceuil vélo" (welcome bikes) certified accommodations throughout the region.

The Tourist Information Bureau will have information and regional maps about bike routes. The maps will indicate forests, vineyards, museums, cave dwellings, villages, and much more. It will also indicate what kind of routes are in which areas. For example, a cycle path that is just for bikes will be indicated on the map by one color, whereas a route shared with cars will be another. The green symbol mentioned above will be posted on places that rent bikes.

A cycling-equipped rest area will be indicated by a bike with a small roof over top, whereas a river shuttle will show a wavy line underneath the image. Roads are also equipped with clear signage for bikes. See, you won't need to know French to bike in France!

Camping

As you spend your vacation in the French Garden, maybe a camping experience would just complete the picture! The French are very fond of camping and many people spend their vacations under the trees, whether in tents, rented cabins or mobile homes, or in their own rigs. As a visitor you, too can rent a cabin, tent, or mobile home. Here are two suggestions for you, one to the east of Tours near Cheverny, and one to the west of Tours, between Saumur and Angers. Some locations offer bike rentals. Otherwise, rentals are likely to be available nearby. For more biking resources, see the biking section on page 164. Remember to book campsites early if you are interested in camping.

Les Saules Sites et Paysages (near Cheverny, east of Tours) offers campsite (called a "pitch"), cabin, or tent (canvas cabin) rental by the week, out in nature. If you don't have a tent or rig, they'll rent you a cabin or a "cabatente" or a wooden tent. Pricing depends on the season and type of accommodation. Early booking discounts are available until June 30. They have packages that include bike rental, access to three nearby châteaux (Cheverny, Chambord, and Blois), and lodging in the cabins.

Of course, you can also easily visit Amboise and Chenonceau and some other local excursions mentioned in the Amboise section of the book. www.camping-Cheverny.com

Camping du Porte Carolina. This campground is located between Angers and Saumur, west of Tours. It is part of a large chain of campgrounds all over France called Flower Campings. You can rent a campsite, a mobile home, a tent (canvas bungalow that holds several people), or a chalet. Covered heated pool, two rivers nearby, and kids' play area increase the enjoyment of your trip. About 250-550€ a week, depending on season and type of accommodation. Open March 31 to September 30. Consult the website for options (there are many!), pricing and reservations as well as more info. www.campingduportcaroline.fr/

Walking and Hiking

There are 6800 miles of trails through the Loire Valley, 374 of which are walking trails. You could say there's something for everyone! There are five well-known hiking trails, called the Grande Randonnée (French for 'the big hike') across the area as well. Twenty-two trails are labeled "Walks in Touraine." Touraine is a word that describes this geographical region all around Tours. The Touraine walks have been set apart for their scenic views, accessibility, and clarity of navigation.

Information on these trails and all amenities for walkers, as well as maps, are available at the Tours Tourist Bureau. Their website is www.tours-tourisme.fr/ You can find a phone number there or get further information.

Boating

Boating, canoeing, and paddle board trips are available on the Loire River and its tributaries, the Vienne, the Indre, and the Cher. The Tours Tourist Bureau office, as well as the Tourist Bureau wherever you are, can help you with this. Check the above link for the Tours Tourism bureau.

Outing boats will take you on a short cruise. There is a list of outing boat companies on the Tours Tourist Bureau link as well. There won't be many long cruises available on the Loire because parts of it aren't navigable except in small crafts.

But you can still get information about renting a self-drive boat for your vacation in one of the waterways nearby. Check www.locaboat.com.

Two more companies to check are LeBoat and French Waterways.

For short river cruises, check the following:

Saumur: River cruise , see page 131.

Blois: Flat bottom boat trip, 4 rue Vauvert, Blois

Chenonceau: sail past the castle in a canoe or a rowboat. See page 92.

Parks and Botanical Gardens

The Loire Valley is itself a kind of garden, but there are also some magnificent gardens and parks to visit, where you'll feel surrounded by nature in a variety of ways.

Here are some opportunities for green space

Food Specialties of the Loire Valley

For more details on wine, see following, page 176-183.

The nickname "the garden of France" is not a random title, but one emerging from the rich, fertile soil around the river itself, and the delicious products that result.

This region is one of France's largest agricultural areas, and *the* largest for organic produce. Here you'll find acres of cheerful sunflowers, providing cooking oil for daily use, along with wheat, barley, and corn, and many other fruits and vegetables, like pears, cherries, lettuce, asparagus, and beets. Mushrooms are cultivated in limestone caves and provide a large percentage of the French supply.

Meals here reflect the bounty of the rich land and rolling hills. If you want to see a list of regional cheeses and wines, the list is very long! Some suggested cheeses you won't want to miss include the most popular, goat cheeses. Some of the best-known are Pouligny-St-Pierre, Crottin de Chavignol, St Maure, and Selle-sur-Cher. Each has a distinct flavor.

A variety of meats, including game, are indigenous to the Loire Valley, and appear in local recipes. Duck, pheasant, pigeon, boar, and rabbit recipes provide a change of pace.

Typical Meals in the Loire Valley

- *Géline de Touraine:* A small hen cooked in the traditional way.
- *Rillettes de porc*, or pork paté, perfect on a slice of baguette or country bread for a picnic. It's also made with salmon and duck, though pork is traditional.
- Desserts: *Tarte Tatin* (upside-down apple tarte), *Sablés* (crumbly butter cookies sometimes flavored with orange or lemon), Plum *Tarte d'Anjou* (note: in French a plum is called a *prune*. A prune is a prune sec, or dried.) Nougat de Tours is an elegant cake made with apricot marmalade and marzipan.
- Fish specialties: Salmon with cream sauce, Zander in butter sauce, eels in wine.

Beverages, what a lengthy topic! First, we have cherry liqueur from Angers, and Cointreau, the famous orange-flavored liqueur also made in the Angers area. You can take a tour of the Cointreau distillery in Angers. Many types of beer are brewed here as well.

In this book there is a more in-depth section on wines of the Loire Valley on page 176, which will give an idea of the types of wines produced in each region.

At one time, this area was more important than Bordeaux for winemaking. The soil in the Loire River valley is rich with nutrients and limestone, which affect all of the produce but creates a very favorable climate for producing wine. The best way to sample a variety of specialties from the Loire Valley is to take a wine tour.

Reds include Gamay from Anjou, Bourgueil, Chinon (from the city of Chinon), Saumur Rouge (from Saumur), Touraine and Coteaux du Loir, among many others.

Among **rosés**, you'll find Rosé d'Anjou, Cabernet d'Anjou, Rosé de Loire and Touraine d'Amboise. Sparkling wines include the famous Vouvray, Crémant de Loire (second only to Champagne in French sparkling wines), and Saumur Brut.

White wines have found their place as well, including the well-known Pouilly-Fumé and Sancerre (which also makes reds and rosés), Saumur Blanc, and Savennière, and of course, Muscadet, which is produced in higher volume than any other wine in the region.

Loire Valley Wines

The only thing more sought-after by tourists (and others) in the Loire Valley than châteaux is *wine*. The Loire Valley is France's most diverse wine-producing region. The region is well-respected as well in France, though less famous outside of France than, say, Bordeaux or Burgundy. Here, many of the wines are produced by smaller vineyards, most of which have been producing Loire Valley wines for generations. More and more wines are produced from organic farms. There are over 3,000 growers, wine cooperatives, and wine merchants in the Loire Valley.

The Romans are given credit for the establishment of wine production in the Loire Valley. Then, given its history as the epicenter for French royalty for centuries and the number of châteaux, many of which had vineyards on the property, it isn't surprising that wine is a primary product of this area. Add to those factors the climate and the limestone soil, favorable for growing grapes.

You may have heard of the AOC system of wine classification in France. What does AOC mean? In the 1930s the French government created the Appellation d'Origine Controllée, which regulates the quality of products such as wine and cheese.

Outside of France, we most often associate the AOC label with wine.

What is an appellation? It is a legally defined and protected *geographical area* that is used to identify where grapes are grown for certain wines. In France the AOC governs what grapes can be used, alcohol levels, ripeness, and other criteria. Despite this requirement, French wine labels are not based on grapes used, but on the *area,* or appellation, where those grapes are grown.

The Loire Valley is the third largest producer of AOC wines in France, and the largest AOC region for white wines. After Champagne, the Loire Valley is the leading producer of AOC sparkling wines and quite a bit of rosé is produced there as well. Wines produced in the Loire Valley are also less pricey than their famous cousins from Bordeaux and Bourgogne (Burgundy.)

Growing regions in the Loire are considered in Lower, Middle, and Upper Loire regions, though depending on what you read, it can be further divided to include upper and central. The Lower Loire region is west of Angers out to the Atlantic coast, including the Nantes area. This area specializes in Muscadet. The upper region would be east and south of Orléans.

The heart of the Loire Valley, which this book covers, is the Middle Loire. Therefore, the wine details that follow will pertain to this area, which includes Anjou in the Angers area, Saumur, south of Angers, and Touraine, which encompasses most of the rest of the territory to the east up to Blois. Anjou and Saumur are often linked together, called Anjou-Saumur.

In terms of grapes, the stars of the Middle Loire are the Chenin Blanc and the Cabernet Franc. This is also the headquarters of sparkling wines, called Crémant.

Middle Loire includes Anjou, Touraine, and Saumur to the west of Tours, and Touraine-Amboise and Cheverny and Cours-Cheverny to the east of Tours. You'll see a lot of sparkling wines around Angers and Tours. Fourteen types of grapes make their way into wines produced in this region. (See below.)

Grapes you'll find in the Loire Valley:

WHITE

- Chenin blanc
- Sauvignon blanc
- Chardonnay
- Arbois (found only in the Loire Valley)
- Pinot Gris
- Romorantin (found only in the Loire Valley, and especially in the Cheverny region.)

178

RED

- Cabernet franc
- Cabernet sauvignon
- Pinot d'Aunis
- Gamay
- Malbec (called Côt in this area)
- Grolleau
- Pinot Meunier
- Pinot Noir

A brief list of some well-known wines from the Loire Valley

Sancerre: A region in the eastern Loire Valley southeast of Orléan. It is an appellation and is known for Sauvignon Blanc. It can be expensive.

Pouilly-Fumé: This wine comes from the area near Sancerre. These wines are also made of Sauvignon Blanc, but less expensive than Sancerre.

Touraine: Wines from this region are generally a good value. They include Sauvignon Blanc, Gamay, Pinot d'Aunis, Côt, and Menu Pinot.

Vouvray: Made only of Chenin Blanc; as well-known as Sancerre, but less expensive. Also available are sparkling wines (crémant) made from Chenin Blanc.

Anjou: Chenin Blanc (mineral, full-bodied), Sauvignon Blanc, Cabernet Franc, Cabernet Sauvignon, Grolleau, Pineau d'Aunis.

Chinon/Borguil, *Saumur/ Saumur-Champigny*: cabernet franc (strong, red, and dominant in this region), cabernet sauvignon, Chenin Blanc. Chinon rosé.

Muscadet: melon de Bourgogne

Bubbly wines: Can be called *Mousseaux*, which, though bubbly, has fewer bubbles than a crémant. A lot of sparkling wine comes from Saumur and surrounding area.

Highlights of the predominant wines of each region

The wines listed are all AOC certified wines.

Anjou

1. Anjou: This region is best-known for fruity rosé wines and red wines. Wine has been cultivated in this area for 1,000 years. Rosé accounts for half of Anjou's production. Some names are: Rosé de Loire, Rosé d'Anjou, Cabernet d'Anjou.

2. Wines produced here include Rosé, Cabernet, Blanc, Rouge, Village, Gamay.

Includes the area called Savannière (known for very good Chenin Blanc.)

3. Sweet wines called Coteaux, Mousseux, and Crémant (which has more bubbles than Mousseux.)

Saumur

1. This is known as sparkling wine country, producing the most sparkling wines in the Loire Valley. When you see the words Crémant or Mousseux, those are sparkling wines.

2. This region also produces red, white, and rosé. A dry Chenin Blanc white is called Saumur Blanc. Saumur Rouge is a spicier red based on Cabernet Franc grapes.

3. Saumur-Champigny is a Cabernet Franc based red wine that some claim is the best in the Loire Valley. (You can taste and decide!)

Touraine

1. This region is the largest, going from Tours to the east, to Blois. It is specifically known for Chenin Blanc and Cabernet Franc grapes.

2. Whites are a blend of Sauvignon blanc and Sauvignon Gris. Reds are likely to feature Cabernet Franc and Malbec (in this region it is called Côt), also with Cabernet Sauvignon, Pinot Noir, and Gamay.

3. There are also sparkling wines, such as Touraine Mousseaux and Touraine Pétillant, as well as Vouvray Pétillant (pétillant means sparkling.)

4. The well-known Vouvray from Chenin Blanc grapes (non-sparkling) also has a strong presence in this region and can be either dry or sweet.

5. This region includes Bourgeuil, Chinon, and Cheverny, among others. Chinon wines are sought-after by wine-lovers. This is especially true of Sancerre (which can be expensive), made from Sauvignon Blanc. Growing nearby are grapes for Pouilly-Fumé and Menetou-Salon.

Each of the regions discussed have numerous vineyards all around, if you are interested in tastings, tours, or more educational events. Some addresses have been suggested in the corresponding sections. To get an overview and more choices, visit the tourist information office in the region where you are staying. They can advise you based on what kind of experience you're looking for and your location. In addition, they can give you a map called *Vins du Val de Loire* (Wines of the Loire Valley), which will show you in color the various appellations in the area. (Similar maps are also available by region.) On the back of the map, you'll see an extensive list of vineyards by region. The Tourist Office can give you recommendations if there are too many to make a clear choice for your visit!

All across the Loire Valley you'll discover excursions surrounding wine harvesting, including hikes through vineyards, visits to the "caves" where the wine if stored, tastings, of course, and thematic events, and festivals. The Tourist Office can advise you on these too.

You can book a tour company for a half or full day (or several days) that will include visits to several vineyards in the area. Most tours take place in small groups. For more information about options for wine tourism in the Loire Valley, check the official website: www.vinsvaldeloire.fr/en

Suggested Itineraries

The following tour ideas can be a starting point for your travels. Hopefully, they will make planning easier, unless you decide to book a tour company that does the heavy lifting for you. Your choice! There are plenty of options.

CASTLE TOUR

Week One: Castle theme (east Loire Valley)

If seeing Loire Valley castles is your top priority, here is a week that will satisfy your craving. This week is full, so you can select your favorites according to your own rhythm.

- Tours (Base here for 4 days) Visit Tours, Langeais, Villandry, and Ussé. If you have time, visit Azay-le-Rideau. Optional: Side trips to vineyard and/or Troglodyte house.
- Amboise: (Base here for 3 or 4 days) Visit town, castle in Amboise. Clos Lucé, Chaumont, Chambord or Cheverny, and Chenonceau. Optional: Side trip to Loches for 1 day *or* a balloon ride.

184

Week Two: Castle theme (west Loire Valley)

- Saumur (Base here 3 days) Visit city and château, Abbey Frontevraud, the town of Chinon, and the Château of Brissac.
- Angers (Stay here 2-3 days) Visit Angers, city and château. Optional side trip to Le Lude and/or vineyard tour.

"BEST OF" TOUR

Week One

The following tour of one or two weeks combines a balance of towns, châteaux, and vineyards.

- Tours (2 days city, 1 day Langeais, Villandry) optional: Vineyard tour
- Amboise (4 days) 1 ½ days Amboise town and 2 days at chateaux, 1 day at Chenonceau and lunch nearby, Montpoupon, if time, on the way to Loches. One day in the town of Loches.

Week Two

- Chinon: 2 days in town, château, and nearby Azay-le-Rideau.
- Saumur: 3 days town, château, vineyard, troglodyte site, and Cadre Noir.

VINEYARD TOUR 8 Days

- Eastern Loire: (Base in Amboise for 3 days.) See castles in Amboise, then head to the vineyards. There are 2 in Amboise itself or if you have a car, you can go a short distance to the towns of Limeray or Chargé. See page 58-59 for listings.

- Western Loire: (Base in Tours for 2 days and Angers for 3 days.) While in Tours, visit one or more of the three vineyards that feature Vouvray wine. If you want to get closer to the earth and really see how it's done, consider a 3-hour tour which takes you into the vineyards themselves, with Rendez-Vous Dans les Vignes (all listings are on page 40 and 41.) While in Angers, visit the town and castle then slip away to the Anjou Vineyards, famous for rosé, but producing red and white too (1 day.) If you'd like something more original, visit the Cointreau Distillery (page 150) near Angers.
Day two: Visit vineyards in and around Chinon (page 106) and stroll around the town.
Day three: Vineyards of Saumur (page 125.) Saumur red wines are very well-known. Visit the town and perhaps the Cadre Noir if you have time.

Vineyards listed in this book are just some suggestions, but the Tourist Information Bureau of each individual town will have many suggestions and recommendations.

NATURE TOUR 8 or more days

If you want to include biking, boating, walking, or all three in your week, consult one of the websites in the corresponding section earlier in the chapter or in the index. There are details in other parts of the book as well.

Many companies offer bike touring packages. They arrange housing and transport of bikes and include several or most meals, as well as entrance to châteaux and other places. One of these is France Today and another is Backroads, which can be for either biking or hiking.

You can arrange a biking circuit for a week and include down times in between where you can be bused from one location to another or rent a small van tour company for a few of your excursions. Be sure to include some vineyard and cave exploration for a varied and fascinating week or two where you'll have the chance to enjoy not only the monuments for which the Loire Valley is most famous, but the lovely surrounding landscape that *is* the French Garden!

CITY TOUR: 8 Days

Maybe you want to prioritize the towns of the Loire Valley, with their unique history and local châteaux. Be sure to check with the Tourist Information Bureau of each town for guided tours where you can learn more about the history of each city and how it is unique in the Loire Valley landscape. This tour can be accomplished entirely by train.

Here are the main towns of the Loire, beginning east and moving west so as not to have to backtrack.

Amboise and Blois: Base in Amboise for 2 nights. Day one, see the town (and château) of Amboise. Day two, see the town and Château of Blois.

Tours: Base here for 4 days. Visit Tours for two days. Then spend one day visiting Chinon and one day visiting Saumur.

Angers: Base here and visit the town for 2 days. One of these can be spent in the surrounding countryside visiting a vineyard or a château, for example, Le Lude or Brissac.

If you have more time available, try to see Loches for 2 days, enjoying the city itself, its château, and the Zooparc de Beauval.

HISTORY TOUR   5 to 8 Days

History buffs, here is your tour! Note that the Tourist Information Bureau can give loads of valuable information on what to see if your focus is history. They will have city tours, and some will have history tours you can take.

Some of the characters and events that are notable in Loire Valley history are mentioned below, but there will be many more to discover.

Amboise: Anne de Bretagne and Charles VIII lived in Amboise. Later, François I invited Leonardo da Vinci. Nearby Chenonceau has its stories involving the lives of Catherine de Medici and Diane de Poitiers, mistress to King Henri II, Catherine's husband.

Chinon: Follow the rise of Joan of Arc and her impassioned plea to Charles VII, which led to the turning point in the Hundred Years War. Cardinal Richlieu later owned the château at Chinon.

Saumur: The castle's history trace back to the counts of Blois and Anjou and continue with the Plantagenet family. Stroll around the town and admire the 15th and 17th century homes.

Angers: The English Plantagenet family, Louis I and the Apocalypse Tapestry. Nearby you'll find the Château de Langeais, which was part of the

Plantagenet family as well, and was the marriage place of Anne de Bretagne and Charles VIII. Châteaux in this area include Angers, Langeais, Le Lude, and Plessis-Bourré. Abbey Frontrevraud, 10 miles from Saumur, is the burial place of the Plantagenet family.

SHORT TOUR: 2 to 4 days total or over a weekend

Tours and Amboise. Visit Tours for one day (or a day and a night) then travel to Amboise. Lodge there 1 or 2 nights and visit the town, 2 châteaux (Amboise and Clos Lucé), and if you have time, you can see nearby Chenonceau.

If one of the above tours doesn't quite fit your objectives, you can use one as a starting point and add or subtract the elements you most want to fit your time frame.

In any case, you have hopefully found enough resources and ideas in this book for many memorable trips to the Loire Valley!

Index

Thank you for purchasing *A French Garden: The Loire Valley*. I hope it's met your expectations. If you have suggestions to offer for future editions or if you find an error or have a question, feel free to contact me at: Info@Oliversfrance.com

If you enjoyed the book and found it helpful, please consider leaving a review so others can discover it too! Thank you!

K. B. Oliver

For more enchanting places to discover in France, check out my travel website, www.Oliversfrance.com. Here you'll find some familiar places as well as some out-of-the way treasures you'd seldom see in other travel books, along with helpful posts about traveling in France. Get a free eBook and 2 monthly posts when you sign up.

Other helpful travel resources

by K. B. Oliver

keep reading . . .

Magical Paris: Over 100 Things to do Across Paris

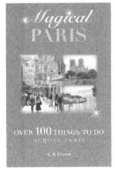

This unique travel book on Paris will help you discover fun things to see and do ALL over Paris (Over 100 of them!), not just in the central, touristy spots. This guide is easy to use and has tons of helpful tips and ideas for your trip, as well as some you won't find anywhere else. It's the easy to use AND carry travel book, with the information you need and not everything you don't!

Real French for Travelers

Book or Online Course

Why would you be satisfied with memorizing phrases you don't understand from a phrasebook when you can learn **real** French? **This book** will help you be operational in French for your next trip. Short, helpful chapters and exercises will lead to confidence in speaking. It's easier than you think!

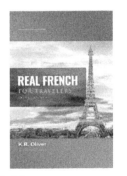

Real French for Travelers is also a **Full-length online course,** which will take you from zero to past tense in easy, concise video lessons. The course is also available as part 1 and part 2, if you'd prefer to start small. Study pronunciation, grammar, and relevant vocabulary for your trip. It's all designed with the traveler in mind. Put away your phrase book and learn REAL French. (20% discount on full course for owners of this book. Use code: LEARNFRENCH at checkout.)

Learn more at www.OliversFrance.com or at www.realfrenchfortravelers.com.

French Greetings and Polite Expressions

Get a head-start on polite French words and expressions with a free online mini-course from Oliver's France. www.Oliversfrance.com. Either scroll down to find the link or consult the Resource tab on the menu.

About the Author

K. B. Oliver lived in France for 13 years, primarily in Paris and its suburbs. Currently she writes fiction and nonfiction and teaches French in North Carolina.

Made in the USA
Coppell, TX
22 May 2022

78057340R00115